STORIES
OF THE
STRANGER

STORIES OF THE STRANGER

ENCOUNTERS WITH EXILES AND OUTSIDERS

Collected by Martin Palmer and Katriana Hazell

Stories of the Stranger

Published in 2014 by
Bene Factum Publishing Ltd
PO Box 58122
London
SW8 5WZ
inquiries@bene-factum.co.uk
www.bene-factum.co.uk

ISBN: 978-1-909657-44-1
Text © Alliance of Religions and Conservation

A CIP catalogue record of this is available from the British Library.

Illustrations: Sylvia Woodcock-Clarke
Book design and typesetting: Ranchor Prime
Cover design: Henry Rivers, thatcover.com
Printed and bound in Malta on behalf of Latitude Press

*Thank you to all the storytellers down through time
who have kept alive the art of the story and the role it has
in broadening, challenging and enthusing our
understanding of our place within the Greater Stories.*

*All royalties raised from this publication will go into
furthering the work of exploring these stories and their
significance for today's strangers and exiles.*

ARC

ALLIANCE OF RELIGIONS AND CONSERVATION
launched in 1995 by HRH The Prince Philip, Duke of Edinburgh KG KT

CONTENTS

STORIES
OF THE
STRANGER

PREFACE

I was three years old when my family moved to Kirkcaldy in the East of Scotland. It was 1954 and the next few years were difficult times. Factories in the area were closing and there was widespread unemployment. My father was the local minister, and throughout my childhood I remember a steady stream of strangers coming to our home asking for help and support. It taught me early lessons about the misery that results from unemployment. But I also saw what people can achieve in the face of poverty when communities are open to helping others when times are hard.

My father was very much a *social* Christian—and his sermons were about charity and good works—and I could see the efforts he made on behalf of others and I will never forget his emphasis on treating everyone as equals. So strangers with problems were always made welcome at our home. They might come with family problems or money problems or because they were lonely or felt rejected. All this coming and going meant my mother, too, welcoming people in, and offering cups of tea. Trying to do my part when my parents were out and I was in the house on my own, I once invited a man in for a cup of tea. I told him to help himself to the food in the kitchen. He turned out to be the most notorious local burglar.

Kirkcaldy is important to our discussion of strangers because it is also the home of Adam Smith, thought by many to be the prophet of modern capitalism, but, in fact, the moral philosopher who was more concerned about our obligations to others.

Visit the town and its one-and-a-half mile long promenade and you will understand how the sea that dominates the town shaped his view of the world. Indeed you cannot understand Adam Smith without understanding the community in which he was born, grew up and to which he returned to in order to write his two great books, *The Wealth of Nations* and *The Theory of Moral Sentiments*.

In Smith's time Kirkcaldy was a major port which specialised in trade between the United Kingdom and the European continent. From his home overlooking the sea, Adam Smith, born the son of the local customs officer, would look out and every day witness some of the hundred or so merchant ships that came in and out of the harbour.

Kirkcaldy flourished by exporting its goods and importing others. This is how Smith came to understand that trade was the engine of growth and that the economy prospered through the specialisation of labour.

But Adam Smith grew up in what was also a strong cohesive community. The church in which he was baptised and the school he attended were but only a few yards from where he lived. And the Adam Smith of "the invisible hand" of free market economics was also the Adam Smith of "the helping hand" of civil society, and indeed, for Smith, his thoughts on moral sentiments were even more important than his theories on the wealth of nations.

He wrote of our capacity to put ourselves in other people's shoes, and thus to consider their interests and needs, and he wrote of the circle of sympathy starting with family friends and compatriots, a sense of obligation that diminished, he recognised, with distance. Understandably we felt less obligations to strangers. But this view was conditional on three forces of far greater importance then than now: our limited knowledge of strangers, our restricted ability to make contact and communicate with them, and our less developed sense of what mutual obligation entailed. If Adam Smith were writing now, he would be showing how distance had ceased to be a barrier to knowledge, how contact and communication with strangers was possible almost instantaneously across the internet, and how, because of our growing interdependence, indeed our dependence on each other, we had developed a stronger sense of mutual obligation. Paraphrasing one American writer, "it is the hands of others who grow the food we eat, sew the clothes we wear, build the homes we inhabit. It is the hands of others who tend us when we are sick and lift us up when we fall. It is the hands of others who bring us into the world and lower us into the grave". If Smith were looking at the world now he might even be writing of us being able to feel, however distantly, the pain of others, and of us being capable of believing in something bigger than just ourselves, and those nearest to us. In this way, those whom yesterday we thought of as strangers, we think of today as neighbours, offering a 21st-century answer to the Biblical question—who is my neighbour?

This book is a collection of rich and deeply moving faith tales and scriptural stories of exile and the outsider. The stories capture, with satire and humour, as well as humility, how we may be more likely to find something profound in the poor exile than in the all-powerful seeming priest. It is an effective and subtle way to show how strangers could become neighbours and how we could all live by the golden rules common to all religions. More often than not, our world can be enriched by strangers—even if we always have to be careful when the local burglar calls.

Gordon Brown
Former Prime Minister of the United Kingdom

INTRODUCTION

They are separated by some four thousand miles. They come from completely different cultures, languages and traditions, and they were both written down about three thousand years ago. What is remarkable is that they agree.

One of the Classics of Ancient China is the Shi Jing, or Book of Poetry. This wonderful compendium of poems from around 1000 BC covers every human emotion, from warfare to love, from the most sublime joy to the deepest sadness. One of the poems (Poem VI in Book Two, part three) tells of the plans of a mighty Prince for a new city for his people:

> The Prince travelled to the place of the hundred springs.
> He viewed the wide plain,
> He climbed the highest hill
> And looked out over the land:
> A land wide enough for many to live there.
> Here there was room to settle,
> Here they could build places for strangers to stay,
> Here he made up his mind:
> This was how it would be.

In Ancient Israel, the Book of Psalms from the same era almost exactly mirrors the Chinese Book of Poetry, and Psalm 146 says the following:

> The Lord is always faithful.
> He protects the persecuted,
> Gives food to the hungry.
> The Lord frees the prisoner.
> The Lord gives sight to the blind,
> Restores those who are crippled.
> The Lord loves righteousness
> And protects the stranger.

Here were two totally different cultures linked by a common concern: namely that the stranger should be cared for and protected and even have special safe places in which to be specially welcomed.

This sentiment runs through all major religions and ancient cultures around the world. It stems not just from the teachings of Holy Books such as the Bible or the Chinese Classics, but also from the stories told down the centuries, down the millennia, about the importance of the stranger.

Both the Bible and the Book of Poetry also contain poems which describe what it is like to be an exile, driven from your own land. In the Book of Poetry there is this ancient and terrible lament:

> I am forever separated from my brothers.
> I call a stranger my father.
> I call a stranger my father
> But he will not look at me.

In the Bible, the Israelites were slaves in Egypt some 3,200 years ago, longing for their freedom:

> I am a stranger in a foreign land… The sons of Israel cried
> aloud in their slavery…and their cry came to God.

The basis of this book lies in this extraordinary historic and sacred fact. That for thousands of years people have seen care for the stranger as a sacred duty, and that for thousands of years people have nevertheless been driven into exile and have wept and sought to understand why this had happened.

This was not, however, the original idea for this book.

It arose originally from a request made to my organisation, the Alliance of Religions and Conservation (ARC), which helps religions develop their own environmental projects. The request came from the Norwegian Government and it was this: could ARC develop a programme with the major faiths which would enable them to respond to the anticipated rise in refugees and migrants triggered by ecological collapse in their home countries?

I replied that we would look into this and so we did.

Many religions and religious organisations are at the heart of helping strangers—be they refugees or simply travellers in need—to find shelter, food and protection. Organisations like the Jesuits and the Quakers have active refugee programmes working in collaboration with the major UN and other refugee agencies. Islamic Relief, Christian Aid and other faith-based development and relief organisations are also active in this field. They didn't need our help so I soon realised that perhaps there was something else we could provide. Something quite unexpected and previously unexplored.

"Immigration fears", "immigration trap", "over-whelmed", "pouring over the border", "taking our jobs": these are all words and phrases used in the media and in discussion about migrants, about strangers in our midst. Warfare, civil unrest, civil war, economic inequalities, and yes, increasingly, environmental degradation in their own countries, have brought millions of exiles and new workers to many countries, and this is creating strains and conflicts with the often resentful resident populations. The rise of anti-immigrant political parties across Europe and within countries such as the USA, South Africa, Australia and many parts of Central Asia is a deeply troubling trend.

It is not just xenophobia, it is also fear of change. I saw that what was being eroded in so many places was a tradi-tional ethos of compassion and care for the stranger, and it was this which made me realise something so fundamental that no one seemed to have really noticed it. I began to realise that every major faith has, at its core, at least one story of exile, of being a refugee or a stranger, and finding kindness and compassion that is transformational. And that through these experiences and stories, told in some cases for thousands of years, came fundamental changes in the self-perception of people and of their understanding of God or of the gods or a divine guiding force.

In Judaism, and later Christianity, this includes the biblical story of the Exodus of the Jews from imprisonment in Egypt and later the Exile of the Jews to Babylon in the 6th century BC. In Islam there is the story of what happened when the city of Makkah, now in Saudi Arabia, turned violently against the early Muslims in around AD 622, and they took refuge with the Christian King of Abyssinia, now Ethiopia. In Hindu India, the key story of exile is the tale of the Ramayana in which the god-King Rama, his brother Lakshmana, and his wife Sita, were forced from their kingdom into exile in the forest.

As I discussed this notion with colleagues and friends from the different religions I began to realise something else. Every culture, indeed every faith, also has stories—folk stories often—about the stranger being somehow a revealer of truths. And about how we are sometimes more likely to encounter the Divine in the stranger, the outcast or the beggar than in the priest, imam, guru or any other official religious or powerful figure.

So, from a single question, began an unusual and unexpected journey: to put together and retell some of the key traditional stories of exile, and of being a refugee and a stranger. I hoped that they would help communities around the world recall that most honourable and increasingly vital insight in their own culture, that the stranger in your midst should be respected and cared for. This should be done for reasons of common humanity and because our most ancient and sacred traditions tell us this is part of what faithful people should do. And because somehow, by reaching beyond what is easy or convenient, we ourselves can be transformed in ways that can give us more extraordinary, richer and, in a different way, better lives.

To do this I went to storytellers from each of the major faiths and asked them to tell me the key stories of exile and of being the stranger. It was a wonderful journey as storytellers from the Baha'i, Buddhist, Christian, Daoist,

Hindu, Jewish, Muslim, Sikh and Zoroastrian religions recounted their stories. Through an evening of storytelling in Nairobi, in Kenya, one night, we were also able to draw in a traditional African story as well as a contemporary one. Through refugees living in the UK we heard stories that helped their own recent experiences make some sort of sense. Each story, while remaining faithful to its origin, has been told for a new audience—you. The result is a fascinating collection of insights into the wisdom and experience of humanity as it has struggled to understand the challenge of the stranger and the shock of exile and of being a refugee. In particular these stories show how this struggle has led to radically new and deeper understandings of the Divine.

The stories are divided into four sections: the first are from the Holy Books such as the Bible or the Buddhist teachings; the second are based on historical accounts which are not from sacred books but are treasured within the faiths as part of their heritage; the third section is drawn from folk stories. These often humorous and vivid stories are fables or stories based upon a historical figure but much enlarged by the storyteller's art. Finally we come to stories of our own time—because never have there been so many strangers in a foreign land, or refugees fleeing warfare and disruption of their homelands.

Each storyteller has taken the essential elements of the story—be that from a Holy Book, from history, from folk legend or from the world of today—and has reworked it in their own distinctive style. This brings a freshness to stories which some might feel they know only too well, while making accessible stories which otherwise might be somewhat lost in the language and style of a more traditional telling.

FROM THE HOLY BOOKS

It was a surprise to discover quite how often in the great Holy Books of the world's faiths, the experience of exile, the challenge of being the stranger and an outcast, was seen as core to a deeper understanding of the Divine.

The Judeo-Christian tradition tells of the Exodus of the Israelites from slavery in Egypt over three thousand years ago and their wanderings through the desert, helped by strangers and their own ingenuity, until they arrived in the Promised Land. Every year Jews around the world celebrate the Feast of the Passover, commemorating the escape of the Israelites from Egypt recorded in the Book of Exodus in the Torah—the first five books of the Bible. Passover recalls for Jews the experience of slavery and the deliverance that God brought when he helped them escape from being "strangers in a foreign land" and brought them home.

Around five hundred years later, in the 6th century BC, the Jews were exiled to Babylon after their kingdom was attacked and conquered by the mighty Babylonian Empire. The tragic poignancy of that terrible period was captured at the time in Psalm 137, which is retold here in the story 'By the waters of Babylon'.

From both of these dramatic events came a wider and deeper understanding in Judaism of who God is. In earlier parts of the Bible, God is seen as their God but with a sense that all the other tribes had their own God. Through the Exile

Judaism came to realise that God is the origin and meaning of all aspects of life for all people, and this has shaped Jewish—and later Christian and Islamic thinking—ever since.

The Christian dimension of this sense of the vulnerability and yet opportunity of learning when you are a stranger is shown in the New Testament story of the family of Jesus and their own exodus soon after he was born. They had to go into exile to escape the murderous intent of King Herod, who had heard that a new king would be born, and sent his soldiers out to kill every first-born boy child under the age of two. That story is told in the Gospel of Matthew, chapter 2: 13–23. Like the Israelites, Jesus and his family took refuge in Egypt where (according to traditional stories not contained in the Bible) they were cared for and protected by the local people. 'And one for our new friend' is set in the time when Jesus and his family had returned from exile and it imagines them encountering a stranger, and learning from their own experience. It deliberately echoes the Exile story insight that God is the God of all people, as a reminder to the followers of Jesus that they must never ever view God as just their God but as the God of all people everywhere.

The ancient Ramayana saga of India, from which so much of contemporary Hinduism takes its inspiration, is all about exile. Driven from his rightful kingdom, Prince Rama accepts that exile is the only peaceful way to deal with the overwhelming greed and ambition of others. And it is in the forest that Rama, his wife Sita, and his brother Lakshmana find the friendships and the strength that will enable them to confront the terrible events of kidnap, warfare and evil which they will encounter later. The title comes from the words of Sita when she learns that her beloved husband Rama is to be exiled: "Then I will go with you"—a response of so many when those they love are driven into exile. Theologically it lays the foundations, in Vedic (Hindu) thought, of devotion and selflessness and provides perhaps one of the two most powerful models of how to understand and respond to evil. The story is inspired by the opening chapters of the Ramayana.

Finally in this section we meet a young prince, over-protected by his parents and living in luxury, who some 2,500 years ago chose to go into self-imposed exile, becoming a stranger to everything he had been taught was important, in order to understand the reality of existence. This extraordinary exile leads to a moment, when this prince, now a recluse who has gone through many journeys to understand how he should live and what the material world really is, achieves enlightenment. The exile was necessary to him earning the right to be called the "Buddha", which means "the Enlightened One". The story of the Buddha is told in 'Even kings know the fear of death'.

These stories have been retold orally and in written form down the centuries. And in this book Emma Geen has retold each of them again.

HISTORICAL FOUNDATION

Not every major faith tradition is as focused on a Holy Book or Books as the Abrahamic faiths of Judaism, Christianity and Islam. For many, the core insights of faith are also contained in stories about their founders or in key moments of their history, recorded not in sacred texts but in the sacred memory and traditions of a people.

Once more, as we went through the process of researching and exploring these historical stories, it took us all by surprise to see how again and again we found stories in which the process of leaving everything familiar became the basis for discovering a new truth. And that truth itself lay in a dimension beyond that which people had previously known and accepted.

This is the basis of 'Many, many moons', which retells the history of the persecution, and then flight of the Zoroastrians from Persia in the 10th century. The same causes lie behind 'The end of the world', which recalls how the founder of the Baha'i faith was sent into exile from Persia (now Iran) in the 19th century, and was put in prison in a remote part of the Ottoman Empire in modern-day Israel. The story of compassion from his jailer reflects core Baha'i beliefs about the spirit of God living within everyone.

In 'Those who will never pass this way again' we have the tale of the founder figure of Daoism in China, Lao Zi, who lived some 2,600 ago. He decided to go into exile because he was disgusted at the lack of morality he saw all around him. He chose to become a stranger, and exile, and to leave all that was familiar. But according to tradition, as he headed towards the West, he was stopped by a sentry at a remote gate-post at the far boundary of the kingdom, and was asked to stay one extra night, and write down his insights before he left. From this, the Dao De Jing (also known as the Tao Te Ching), one of the shortest sacred books in existence, comes the core teachings of Daoism.

In 'Not for a mountain of gold' we hear the story of the earliest followers of Islam who fled from persecution in Makkah and found sanctuary and protection with the Christian King of Abyssinia. It is a story of trust, and of understanding what is most important in the world, and one which has formed the foundation of good relationships between Christians and Muslims even in the most difficult of times. It is why, when extremists attack churches in Muslim countries, as has happened for example in Syria or Egypt in recent years, many Muslims will go out to protect the churches from such attacks.

In 'Feasting by faith' we have a story from the traditional culture of Africa, which captures yet again how the stranger and our response to the needs of the stranger can lay the foundations for a greater understanding of who we are.

FOLK STORIES AND LEGENDS

My middle name is Giles and from my early years the story of that saint has been an inspiration for me—I'd go so far as to say it has shaped the very work I do. "Giles was a wealthy Greek aristocrat," my mother would tell me. "But when his parents died, leaving him a fortune, he decided to give all that money to the poor, left his homeland and travelled to a remote part of France where he became a hermit deep in a forest. One day he heard in the distance the sound of royal hunting horns, and suddenly into the clearing in front of his cave ran a young hind, a female deer. A hunter was so intent upon the chase that even though Giles was standing beside the terrified deer, he shot an arrow. Giles placed his arm in front of the deer and took the arrow destined to kill her into the back of his own hand. The hunter turned out to be the crown prince, who was so moved by Giles' courage in protecting the creature, that he sent his doctors to heal him. When he became king, he would often visit the hermit in his cave, to learn from him and discuss important matters and become a wiser, and a better king. And from then on, the animals in that forest at least, were protected."

With that as "your" story, how could you not want to live up to it, and dedicate your life to protecting nature?

Folk stories, about holy people, or people going on journeys, or even entirely mythological figures who make brave decisions, are often more powerful than even the sacred texts from the Holy Books. These stories have been told and retold in families around fires, at festivals in costumes and masks, and in market places for many centuries and have become some of the most beloved of stories. And once again, when we turned to look at them, we found that many of these folk stories have as a central feature, the importance of the stranger as a recurring theme. Take the legend of my other saint, Martin, in the story titled 'Oh, it's good to see you'. Martin was a soldier, and when he saw a beggar by the roadside he gave him half of his cloak. That night Jesus came to him revealed in the form of the beggar. The story is a powerful illustration of one of several teachings in the New Testament about acts of kindness to an outsider (Matthew, chapter 25: 31–46) in which Jesus says: "when I was a stranger, you made me welcome".

Many of these folk stories are funny. 'My clothes were welcome' tells one of the many, many comic Islamic stories of Mullah Nasrudeen, someone who lived probably in the 13th century AD and around whom stories have gathered. It tells of the banning of the Mullah from a feast, when he looked like a poor man, and contrasts it with his welcome when he returns in his best clothes, highlighting the superficiality of judging people by their outward appearance.

In 'That's just my laundry', the stranger has the last laugh on someone who tried to pretend she had nothing to offer a stranger, while in the 'What on earth has happened' story we meet a dashing matinée-idol Daoist who learns the hard way that beauty is not the key to truth and wisdom. Both show the wonderful fun of seeing the pompous getting their comeuppance.

The theme of the other two stories in this section is how things that are apparently insignificant can sometimes be the most important. In 'All the riffraff' we meet the Greek Orthodox saint Philaret and his exasperated wife. Philaret sees Christ in everyone (particularly those in need), while his wife expresses her frustration at how he keeps inviting all these people into her nice house—until she too finds that helping the stranger, the beggar and the outcast is actually a way to real happiness. In the powerful 'A crack in the wall', we hear the story of a humble Hindu pilgrim, Kanakadasa, whose only thought is how he is going to see Krishna, so much so that as he reaches the front of the queue, he trips. Which brings on the wrath of the temple priests. This story walks a path familiar in many cultures: that when those who set themselves up as the guardians of the Divine get it wrong and turn away the beggar, the poor person, the stranger, then the Divine will in turn react, and challenge the religious elite right back. These stories all tell us that no-one is more important, whatever their social status or wealth.

MODERN

The past hundred years have seen more people driven into exile by violence in their homeland, or by severe economic inequalities, than any time in human history. The rise of nationalism in the 19th and 20th centuries led to millions being driven from their homes because they were of the wrong ethnic or religious background. 'The Promise' tells of the horrors and heartache of one such ethnic cleansing when, after the disastrous Greek-Turkish War of 1919–1922, the city of Smyrna was occupied and the Greek population fled. The settlement which ended the war led, in 1922 and 1923, to the wholesale exchange of perhaps as many as three million people—of Muslims living in what is now Greece and Greek Orthodox Christians living in what is now Turkey. There are, as a result, more than three million stories we could have found—from the people exiled, and the people staying in places suddenly full of strangers—and we have chosen one from our storyteller, Anna Conomos, that was inspired by oral testimonies, photos and folk stories from Asia Minor. She wrote and performed the story as part of the exhibition about forced migrations in the 20th century, 'Twice a Stranger'.

'So strange' tells a moving story of double exile and of three strangers. Set in the confusion and chaos of Partition, when British India was split into Muslim Pakistan and Hindu India, it tells of the Sikhs caught in between. But in particular it tells of a severely handicapped child who is abandoned outside a Sikh temple—a total stranger—and who is adopted by one of India's most remarkable men.

'The Lion' tells of how those who leave their homelands and arrive in a strange land can encounter a loss of identity, as people ("aliens" is the official term) whose customs are not valued. Based on the experience of the Jewish communities of Ethiopia, Jews who had lived in Ethiopia for centuries, if not millennia, it not only tells a story of loss of communal activities but is a parable about the danger of trying too hard to please your new neighbours.

'Sister Agatha's mobile' is a true story told one night by a Catholic Nigerian nun (called, of course, Sister Agatha) at a storytelling session we organised during a meeting of African religious environmental leaders in Nairobi in September 2012. It reminds us that—just as former British Prime Minister (and son of the Manse) Gordon Brown describes in his preface—not everyone who turns up as a stranger asking for help is necessarily good. The theological challenge with which his story, and Sister Agatha's, confronts us is that it is better to be mistaken than to refuse compassion. The cost of kindness is that sometimes it will be abused. But to not be compassionate to the stranger for fear of being tricked is to choose the worst of two possible paths.

And finally, 'The shadow of shame' is a morality tale from Korea. It tells about greed and need, and about what it takes to shame someone into recognising that the stranger is as much part of our community as our friends. It is timeless because it tells a core truth. It is timely because the attitude of exploitation, resentment and fear of the stranger is growing around the world, as the number of exiles and refugees increase.

We hope that through all these stories we can remind ourselves and the great faiths and cultures of the world that we should welcome the stranger. Not just because it is the good thing to do, but also because it is the only thing to do. And who knows? We could learn something ourselves.

Martin Palmer
Secretary General of ARC

PART ONE

FROM THE
HOLY BOOKS

1

THEN I WILL GO WITH YOU

Emma Geen

The title of this story comes from the crucial moment when Sita, the wife of the rightful heir to the throne of the Indian kingdom at the centre of the Ramayana decides to join her husband in exile.

The Ramayana is one of the two great epics of India—the other being the Mahabharata. The story of the Ramayana has been told and retold for millennia. No one knows how old it is. Some Hindu teachers say it is ten thousand years old; textual evidence seems to suggest that it was written down around 2,500 years ago. However it is likely that it circulated as an oral tradition for a long time prior to that date, which is why we have placed it as the first story in this opening section, as its oral version at least probably predates the other stories.

"Ramayana" means "Rama's journey". But the journey the eponymous hero goes on is not just the physical journey of exile from his beloved kingdom. It is not just about wandering through the forests with his wife and brother and then in the later part of the story travelling to the Kingdom of the Ten-Headed Evil God Ravana to free his wife Sita from captivity. It is also an inner spiritual journey through which he and those with him discover their own strengths and learn through the experience of exile how precious it is to show friendship to the stranger.

3

Long warm days I sit with my brother and his wife by the chuckling river, sun caught in my eyelashes as I watch the whooper swans court amongst white lotus. Though I never thought I'd say it, we are happy in the forest. Yet even in this wild paradise I cannot stop the image from creeping like winter into my heart.

It is always the same. I am kneeling in a cavernous throne room, its dark walls enmeshed with loss like a spider's web. A pair of empty sandals sits on the throne. Fourteen years must pass until they are filled again.

Outside a cold wind howls down the empty streets. Only one word can be heard in its hollow despair.

Rama.

It was the day of the coronation. The streets rang with the joy of the crowd, everyone clamouring to catch a glimpse of their prince on his way to the palace. Those lucky enough to push to the front saw a chariot of gleaming gold and jewels, though such finery could not outshine the glory of my brother who stood at its helm, his eyes glowing with the red of the divine and his skin the pure blue of summer sky. Prince Rama, heart of Ayodhya. Next to him in the chariot I smiled and lifted my head to the path of the morning sun.

It was Sumantra, not father, who met us at the palace. The shade and quiet was welcome after the jostle of the crowds so we weren't overly concerned at the lack of ceremony. Even Sumantra's grave expression couldn't sour our good mood as we followed him to Kaikeyi's bedroom.

In the strong light, at first I only saw the hard silhouette of Kaikeyi at the window. Rama however drew a sharp breath.

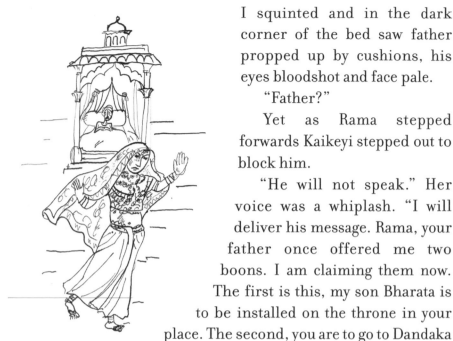

I squinted and in the dark corner of the bed saw father propped up by cushions, his eyes bloodshot and face pale.

"Father?"

Yet as Rama stepped forwards Kaikeyi stepped out to block him.

"He will not speak." Her voice was a whiplash. "I will deliver his message. Rama, your father once offered me two boons. I am claiming them now. The first is this, my son Bharata is to be installed on the throne in your place. The second, you are to go to Dandaka forest. There you will live as a hermit for fourteen years." Her eyes were flinty arrowheads. "You know your father promised my father that my son would be king."

The blood was beating so hot in my ears that I barely caught all of that evil speech. Yet Rama didn't even flinch. He's in shock, I thought and prepared to leap to his defence, but before I could he spoke.

"If father has given you his word then I must respect his promise. I will leave for Dandaka this day."

Now it was I who was truly stupefied. By the time I had recovered Rama was already out of the room.

"You're really doing this?" I yelled as I chased him down the corridor but he didn't answer, just kept walking, his strong back moving steadfast ahead of me, head held as high as ever. Perhaps he is in shock, I thought to myself.

"You will bow to such treason?"

"It is my sacred duty." There was no heat in his voice, no emotion at all.

At the exit to the courtyard, I slipped past him and blocked the doorway.

"You can't do this. I won't let you."

A thin line pinched his brow. "Would you have me disobey our father?"

I beat the wall with my fist but even the iron glow of my fury couldn't kindle a spark in his heart. Rama is too good, always has been. In a world of demons and base mortals there are those that would exploit a man like him. Sometimes it falls to me to understand for him.

"Rama. The emperor has gone mad. Better kill him than be banished."

At those words his eyes finally flamed but the anger was for me.

"Listen to yourself. The Lakshmana I know would not speak so."

And he pushed past me and exited the palace on foot.

"Trust is the source of our strength," he told me when I drew level again but I knew he was still angry as he spoke without even looking at me. "Understand this. I would rather live in the forest owning nothing more than the clothes on my back than rule at the price of my honour."

"But Kaikeyi—" I hissed.

"It is not her doing. Father and his wife are under the

control of providence. I accept it as the will of the gods."

Even though there was some truth in his words my mouth remained stale with the paste of anger. Stubborn. Stubborn. Stubborn. No man has ever bested Rama in combat but sometimes he is his own worst enemy.

The walk to Sita's took ten times longer than it should have. The terrible news had swept through the city like wildfire, driving people into the street, their faces shining with tears.

"We will follow you," they cried to my brother. "The whole city will follow you so that the forest becomes Ayodhya and Ayodhya reverts to forest."

I shot Rama a meaningful look but he would hear nothing of it. It was only upon entering Sita's chamber that he began to shake. He lowered his head to her fair shoulder and hope lit in my chest. Theirs is a love as deep and strong as the Ganges. Rama could never leave her. I was sure of it.

Yet on hearing his story she didn't faint or cry but simply sighed into his chest.

"Then I will go with you."

It was then that I knew the whole of Ayodhya had gone mad.

"Sita, in the forest you will find only hardship and demons. You shall have none of your staff or finery, only the hard ground and cruel weather to serve you."

Despite the tragedy she almost smiled at me.

"As a young girl, I once heard a wise woman tell my mother that one day I would live in the forest." She held Rama's face between her hands and stared up at him, her eyes as brilliant as the moon on a dark night. "It is my destiny to follow Rama."

At this Rama lifted her with a laugh of delight. Yet in their joy I could hear premonitions of their dying screams. The two of them have never known anything but the finest comforts our kingdom can offer, how can they live as hermits? I seized Rama's arm.

"If you will take Sita then you must agree to take me, too. We have never been separated, we can't part for fourteen years."

He drew me into his and Sita's embrace. "Then so be it. Let the three of us make our new home in the forest."

I had meant to stop the madness in its tracks but in that moment I wondered if I had only fuelled it.

When the time came to leave, our three had swollen into a weeping crowd that chased Rama's chariot, determined to make him see sense. Yet their pleas only drove him to urge the horses on faster. As I watched the proud city walls dwindle, I felt as if my left leg had been tied to the city and the right to the chariot. I was being torn in two. Rama, though, didn't spare a backward glance.

It was an hour before he realised the state of the poor citizens straggling behind us and dismounted to continue on foot. By the time we reached the River Tamasa, the evening was falling, so we stopped and sought what little rest the night could offer us. My thoughts were too enflamed to sleep so I sat with Sumantra by a small fire and spat the embers of my anger. How were Rama and Sita to survive in the wilderness? In that moonless night I really believed that my brother was walking to his own death. Yet when he came to my campfire and gestured, I followed without a word. We slipped away through the sleeping crowd, across the river and into the forest.

The days that followed were plagued by fears that feasted on my thoughts like the mosquitoes on me. Yet standing at last on the high slopes of Chitrakoot, I breathed in the sweet air and the knots of my muscles began to loosen. Sita seemed similarly comforted. As we looked at each other, we knew that this would be our new home.

We built three small huts of leafy branches and an altar to burn a sacred fire. The trees lavished us with a feast of syrupy papayas and mangoes, pomegranates whose skin cracked onto jewelled seeds, as clear and red as the light of Vishnu's eyes. And so we lived in tranquillity, the agony of our loss balmed by bright birdsong and vibrant colour. If this is exile, I thought, then perhaps it's not so bad.

We had not been settled for many weeks when Rama heard the distant roar of elephants. His ears have always been better than mine. I climbed a tree and gazed out. Beneath a cloud of dust, a vast army moved through the valley below. There were hundreds of archers in chariots and elephants decorated in sprays of splendour.

"Put out the fire." I cried down to Rama. "Fetch our bows. It is a whole army."

Yet Rama was not perturbed.

"Can you see who it is?"

I squinted and saw a banner thrust above the treeline that proudly bore the white trunk and silver leaves of Ayodhya. It was Bharata.

My bellow disturbed a cloud of birds from the canopy.

"Let's kill him and his evil mother. Then you can rule, Rama."

"I have given my word." Rama's voice rose up from the forest floor, hardened with disapproval, "but if you wish, I will ask Bharata to give the throne to you."

It was a cruel reproach. Rama knows I've never wanted anything but the best for him. The fight left me and I slipped back down the tree, face lowered to hide my shame.

Yet he was right, when Bharata entered the clearing and ran at Rama, his cries were full of sorrow not war. As they embraced, I stood back, fingering my bow.

"Please believe me," Bharata told Rama. "I did not ask mother to do as she did. The throne is yours. Return home and I will live fourteen years as an ascetic in your place."

Rama stopped him with a raised hand. "I have my fate and you have yours. Listen to Father's counsel and you will rule wisely."

But at that Bharata only lowered his head. We didn't need to ask. Rama had been the light of Father's life. I leant on my bow, heart dislodged into my throat.

Rama was hoarse when he finally spoke. "With Father gone, there really is nothing remaining to me in Ayodhya. I cannot return."

At least Bharata had the good sense to argue against this. The two of them debated until the sun had journeyed across the sky. I hoped Bharata could speak sense into Rama where I had failed, yet it was not to be. The tears were burning in my eyes when Bharata at last gave up.

"Then I will govern until your fourteen years are over and you can return as emperor. But until then—" He reached into his robes and pulled out a pair of simple wooden sandals which he placed on the ground. "Put your feet upon these and they will be installed on the throne as a reminder of the true emperor."

Rama did and Bharata swept them up. Then, with no more words to soften the tragedy, Bharata marshalled his army. Rama, Sita and I watched them slip back into the trees, until the clearing was filled only with silence and an absence as thick as stone.

2

BY THE WATERS OF BABYLON

Emma Geen

In 586 BC the Babylonians captured and destroyed Jerusalem at the end of a long period of resistance by the Israelites (as the Jews were known then) and the survivors of the siege were taken away into captivity in Babylon as punishment. There, beside the river of Babylon, they were put to work. It was not until 538—forty-eight years later—that they were allowed to return to Jerusalem when Babylon was captured by the Persian King Cyrus.

This traumatic period of Jewish history produced perhaps the most dramatic rethinking of who God was and what God's relation-ship was—not just to the Israelites as a tribe but to the whole of the world. In the pre-Exile period, this earlier belief is reflected for example in Psalm 86 that states: "Among the gods there is none to compare with you, no great deeds to compare with yours" (verse 8). The Israelites saw their God as just that, as their God, while other tribes and peoples had their own gods.

The Psalms—from which this story is drawn—are ancient poems from the rich history of the Israelites, stretching back millennia, and many of them were written during the Exile period as prayers and cries of pain and distress.

The overthrow of their way of life left the Israelites bewildered. They felt betrayed and confused. What had happened to their protector God? Had they so offended Him that He had deserted them? In which case what sort of God was He? This question is raised in psalm after psalm (Psalms 79 and 83 are good examples). "Why has this happened?" they ask again and again.

In grappling with this the Israelites began to believe that their God was actually the only God and that all of history, all of life, was under His guidance and sway. For the first time, the texts from this Exile period reflect this vision of a God who is the ruler and maker of all, not just the God of the tribe of Jacob, Joseph and Moses.

In trying to bring home the significance of the Exile, the artist Sylvia Woodcock-Clarke has chosen to depict the Israelites in captivity in the clothes of the Nazi concentration camps. The Shoah— Holocaust—of the Nazi era also threw up huge questions of meaning and of the nature of God's relationship to human life and fate. These questions are still being explored, not only by Jews but by those whose predecessors caused this terrible persecution—namely the Christian countries which were the sites of these camps and murders.

T he air of exile should not taste so sweet. From the shores where we sit I can see the lush heads of trees, sparkling waterways and thick fields of barley lit gold beneath the saccharine sky. Watching over all this is the sandy crest of the heathens' ziggurat, an omnipresent reminder that this is but a parody of home. "The devil's paradise," Isaiah says. Amongst all this beauty we are as naked as Adam in Eden.

About me, what is left of the daughters of Zion huddles together to merge tears in the yellow dust, our faces downcast, like the branches of the trees we sit beneath that trail in the river.

"Remember the temple—"

"Such beauty—"

"Watching the sunset over Zion—"

A thin wail bursts from the murmurs to stab the heavens. It is Esther, the only one of her family to escape the slaughter. It was better in the desert where the air throbbed with our anger and the burnt dust tasted of the ashes of our homes. Sometimes I'd rather we had died than had the heart torn from our chests. For even as Yahweh forgets us we shall never forget Jerusalem. I let my head bow to my lap. In the dark our sighs merge with that of the rushing water. At least the river weeps.

The memories become dimmer and more urgent with every passing day, and so I strive to play them across the back of my eyelids like old Noam would make the shadows of beasts and birds from his hands by the fire. I clench my eyes until I find the throngs of uplifted faces that shone with the light of the Lord as my fellow Levites and I filled the sky with song.

> Yahweh said to me, "You are my son.
> Today I have become your father.
> Ask of me, and I will give the nations for your inheritance,
> The uttermost parts of the earth for your possession.
> You shall break them with a rod of iron.
> You shall dash them in pieces like a potter's vessel."

Yet in the end it was the promise that shattered. Now Noam's hands are pecked at by the birds they once gave life

to. Not just him. Elijah. Freda. Ephraim. Jeremiah. Marni. Too many names to hold on one tongue alone and so we whisper them together. These are our only songs now.

At a rattle of breath I lift my head. It is Ezekiel, the skin of his hollowed face like stretched parchment. I wave away the fly that cleans itself atop his cracked lip. He will not last the day unless he drinks yet he refuses these foreign waters. I gaze into the dark hole of his slack mouth. Where once sprung praises to God lies only a tongue shrivelled as a riverbed in drought. Light catches in my eye and for a second I see myself as a boy that relentless summer when the Jordan shrunk and I slipped my father's hand to race to the writhing sun. I had thought it the fire of Yahweh but instead I stumbled across silvered fish, flailing and gasping at the air they could not breathe. Did they feel the same fist as that around my chest? Did they carry the same stone in their hearts?

I look to my harp at my feet. The sun glistens from the ridges of its black horns curving into the gleaming wood yet it too is as stone, the strings but dried sheep guts. For what praises can be sung in foreign lands? What God is there to hear? Instead the laughter of our gaolers fills the air.

I glare up at the closest, a short ugly man, the alien's thick hair curling over his hide like a pig.

Seeing me look, he approaches, booming between blackened teeth.

"Play for us." I glare at the spread of his thick hands and give him the heat of my eyes. He tugs me up by the shoulders.

"Sing."

His breath is sour with the sweat of alcohol. I curl my lip. The only song I would sing for you is praise of your head shattered across a rock.

He leers and stoops to grab my harp. My hands smart as he shoves it into them.

"Sing for us. Sing a song of Zion."

As if beasts could understand the language of the Lord. There is no song in my heart, even should I wish to find it. I stand numb, staring at my chaffed hands wrapped around the sounding chamber. Dead fingers to dead wood. I see it clearly now. So let tree return to tree. I walk past the man to the nearest poplar and reach up to hook the strap over the lowest branch.

The shadow of the pig's hand falls across my face but

before he can hit me the brilliance of my expression turns his head. My brothers are stood about him as one. Harps in hand, they step forwards and hang them in the trees.

The merriment has burnt from his charcoal eyes. The hand he thought to land against my cheek has closed into a fist. I wonder then if they will kill us and my chest heaves, not for fear of death but at the idea that my blood should soak into this alien soil, so far from Zion and the graves of my ancestors. I read the Lord's name on my lips, chest thrust forwards for the blade but then the man throws his head back and howls.

"They think they are birds." He turns to his friends,

snorting the words between bellyfuls of laughter. "Birds that sing in trees."

The beasts bark their merriment, clutching each other and slapping hands to thighs. Two spread their arms and swoop in circles round me, chuckling like the bulbul bird. Then the first grabs my nose so hard that I know there will be a bruise there in the morning.

"You have a beak but where are your wings? How do you think to fly home to Jerusalem without?" He bows his fore-head to mine like a brother giving advice, though the hiss is anything but. "You are not a bird but the worm that eats the dirt." And throws me to the ground.

I lie there, mouth dry with dust and hatred, watching his sandals move away. The toes between the leather straps are fleshy but I know in truth they are cloven.

When he is gone Dara rushes to me but I shirk from her touch and stride down to the bank, fists so tight that the nails cut into my palms. Let my hands wither before I forget Jerusalem. Let my tongue cleave to the roof of my mouth if I do not count it greatest of my joys.

I step into the river until it laps around my calves. The quiet is filled by the weeping river and the lilted sigh of the breeze fingering a hundred strings—a hollow abandoned sound. I clench my eyes against the rising tears. Ezekiel will not take from the waters of this land I shall not give to them. Yet in that moment a memory of the Gihon spring fills my ears and a tear squeezes from the corner of my eye. I remember its waters chuckling down into the Kidron Valley, the crops that supped from them, the harsh eye of the sun that lapped them up. The tear runs into the hollow of my cheek. I remember the fresh rainfalls that swept across

Judah, the thick clouds that billowed on towards the Dead Sea. All waters join in the end. I let the tears fall freely and watch the river carry them away.

3

EVEN KINGS KNOW THE FEAR OF DEATH

Emma Geen

The story of how a pampered prince called Siddhartha Gautama became the Enlightened One—in Sanskrit "The Buddha"—is set around 550 BC in northern India. When the crown prince was born there was a prediction that he would either be a great ruler or a great teacher. His father wanted a great ruler as a son, and so sought to prevent the boy from knowing that there was anything to teach about. He ordered that Siddhartha should be brought up closeted away from anything which could disturb his peace of mind, and that there should only be delightful, beautiful, uncomplicated things in his life.

This episode from Siddhartha's story tells of how the prince comes to realise that life is more complex than just pleasure and that indeed pleasure can be the trap which prevents us from escaping from the reality of suffering and leading us towards enlightenment. The realisation that his life up until then had been an illusion led the Prince to go into voluntary exile in the forest leaving behind his wife and young son and all the wealth and delights of palace life. Only through this exile from all that was normal for him could he find truth.

Prince Siddhartha wanted for nothing, if by nothing one means anything material. He had a good marriage and a healthy son, an army of servants, stables full of horses, enough gold and jewels to set his three palaces sparkling, not to mention the most decadent of foods and wines. Few men to have walked this Earth have owned more, yet as Siddhartha moved through his vast halls he would listen to the thin echo of his footsteps and feel that there should be something more.

When he turned twenty-nine, Siddhartha called his charioteer with the intention of meeting his subjects. Beneath the jubilant sun, the red earth buildings of Kapilavastu glowed like fire and the beautiful faces of the citizens shone. Basked in this glory, for a fleeting moment Siddhartha felt satisfied with life. Yet it was in this moment that he glimpsed a strange creature lurking in the shadow of a building. The chariot was halfway down the street before he recovered enough to cry out.

"Your Highness?" The charioteer baulked as he yanked the horses to a halt. "What is the matter?"

"Channa—" Siddhartha gasped, for that was the charioteer's name. "I saw a creature. It looked like man but...it had skin like an elephant's. Its arms were like twigs and its back was as crooked as a branch. And silver hair, as silver as the horse's tackle."

The charioteer stared down the street, his face wide with fear, but as Siddhartha watched, Channa's expression creased into perplexity.

"You mean him?" he said, pointing.

Siddhartha whisked round and caught sight of the odd creature. Now that they had slowed he could see that it had not been lurking but that its legs were so feeble that it had to lean against the wall to walk. Inch by inch it was dragging itself towards them, its expression splintered in pain. Siddhartha's skin crawled. What poor creature was this, so pathetic that it wasn't even sovereign of its own body?

"Your highness, that is but a man." Channa told him.

"A man? You're telling me that that creature is human?"

"My prince, he is merely very old and infirm."

"Old?" Siddhartha twisted his tongue around the odd taste of the word. "What do you mean?"

The charioteer could no longer hide his amazement. At Siddhartha's birth holy men had prophesied that the prince would either grow into a powerful king or turn from this life to become a great spiritual leader, and wishing to ensure the former, the King had sheltered his son from knowledge of human suffering. This was widely known amongst the servants of the palace. Yet Channa had never imagined that Siddhartha could be ignorant to such an extent.

"When a man has lived many seasons upon this earth he begins to slow and change."

"Everyone?" Siddhartha almost choked on the word. "You are saying that I will become like that *thing* in time?"

That moment of silence, as he stood trembling in anticipation for Channa's reply, was one of the worst of his life.

"But, is there no way of preventing it?" He stuttered when it became clear that no answer would come.

The charioteer twisted his leather reins. His hands were calloused and rough with hard work but the eyes he lifted to his master's were as vulnerable as a child's. "Life is suffering."

These words fell on Siddhartha like a physical weight.

He, like any man, knew the meaning of pain; despite the attentions of his father he had experienced grazed knees as a child, but he had never imagined suffering could exist on such a scale.

He shaded his eyes from the burn of the sun, finding himself suddenly queasy.

"I'm not well. Take me home."

Siddhartha had hoped to forget the old man, yet the more he tried to force the image from his mind, the more it haunted him. As he walked through the palace, the memory of that emaciated creature rang out with his every hollow footstep, chasing him from room to room.

Old.

One day, like unruly horses, these legs would refuse his weight.

Old. Old.

One day this back, the back of a prince, would bow to the winds of time.

Old. Old. Old.

There would be no rest until he had explored the matter further. He called Channa and set out into the city once more. This time he saw someone the charioteer called "sick", a form of suffering that could befall anyone, no matter how few or how many years they had spent on the earth. Hearing this, the horror Siddhartha had experienced upon seeing the old man doubled in his guts. To suffer after time was bad enough but for some to suffer longer and more cruelly than others seemed beyond unfair. Though the chariot was of sturdy wood and metal, Siddhartha felt as if the ground was giving beneath him.

Old. Sick.

Back in the embrace of his palace he repeated these new terrible words. All these years, whilst Siddhartha had enjoyed riches and good health, people in his city had suffered without his even knowing. Seeking comfort, he summoned his servants to bring him his finest gold and jewels, yet as he gazed upon them he only saw the dull reflection of his fearful face. He had to journey into the city again.

This time Siddhartha saw a group of people weeping over a prone man. He is sick, Siddhartha thought to himself and dismounted, questions readied on his tongue. As he stepped through the crowd he saw that the sickness had eaten the flesh from the man's face leaving it sallow and yellowed. He reached out to smooth the tortured brow but Channa caught his arm.

"My prince, do not disturb the dead."

"Dead?" Siddhartha's echo came out as a whisper. Though he had never heard the word he could see its seriousness on the faces surrounding him. Was this 'dead' the worst suffering of them all?

"All men die, my prince. It is—" Channa's mouth moved silently as he struggled to find an explanation. "It is a sleep from which no one wakes."

Never wake? All men?

Siddhartha grasped the charioteer for support, as if he had been struck as feeble as the old man. The city was bled of colour on their return to the palace. Even the laughter of the children that chased their chariot seemed to hide tears.

"What is it?" his wife asked him when she woke that night to see Siddhartha bowed at the edge of their bed. Her melodic voice, muffled with sleep, kindled warmth in his thoughts, but when he looked back at her silhouette in the dark, he saw a visage of the corpse. One day "age" would steal the colour of her hair and eat the plump flesh of her beautiful cheeks. One day his wife would die.

He rose from the bed before the sun and called for Channa. Old age, sickness, death, there had to be an answer to such suffering. As they set out into the dawn, he drooped against the side of the chariot, his limbs weak but eyes as wide as a man compelled. Into this bleak state there flashed a shock of colour and Siddhartha looked down to find himself staring into the clear eyes of a man sat upon a reed mat. The man was naked save for a rag around his loins and the bright paints upon his face.

"He wasn't old, or sick or dead, I don't think." Siddhartha mused after they had passed. "Yet there was something strange about him."

Channa bit his tongue before replying. Out of fear of the prophecy, the King had sought to hide religion from Siddhartha as well as suffering. Yet the charioteer could not ignore the pleading of his master's eyes. "He was an ascetic. An ascetic is someone who has renounced the world, seeking release from the fear of death and suffering."

At this, a firefly of hope lit in Siddhartha's heart. So there was a way to escape the horror of mortality! He almost embraced Channa in his joy.

When they returned that night, Siddhartha found that young women had been ordered to dance for his pleasure but where before he had beheld only beauty, now he saw the sweat glistening on their faces and the weariness in their steps. By the end of the performance his decision had made itself. He left the palace the next day.

And so Channa drove him to Rajagaha. There they lived as mendicants, begging for alms in the street. Though the riches of his youth had swaddled his senses like a baby, in the raw elements Siddhartha came to know the grip of real existence. And so, just as Channa had taught him the meaning of old age, sickness and death, now he learnt the fundamental meaning of hunger, exhaustion and bodily discomfort. Whereas in his palaces the nights had been made of sweet caresses, in the street cold dug its talons as deep as bone. Whereas as a prince hot days had been cooled by servants working fans, as a mendicant the sun seared and a drone of flies drank from his sweat. Within a week his palaces seemed to him like figments woven of cloud.

Yet whilst he had forgotten royal life, it had not forgotten him. King Bimbisara of Rajagaha had heard of Siddhartha's disappearance and when his men reported seeing the prince begging, he went to talk to him. At first he couldn't comprehend that Siddhartha's exile was truly self-imposed. Why would a prince willingly leave his riches and power behind? Other royalty had waged wars to prevent such a fate. Yet as he listened to Siddhartha, his disbelief turned to awe. After all, even kings know the fear of death.

King Bimbisara's white trousers kissed the red dust and, bowing his head, he offered Siddhartha his throne. Yet the mendicant just smiled. He had learnt much since the day he had first seen an old man. He knew now that a throne could not slow the passage of time, that jewels can't cure a man of his sickness and that, even were every kingdom on earth to marshal its armies, death could not be inflicted a single wound. Most importantly, he understood that everyone becomes an exile before the end, an exile from the dearest home of all, that of his body. And so Siddhartha politely refused the King's offer, requesting only that he and his men leave him to his peace.

When they had gone, Siddhartha lifted his head to the clear sky. A single bird traced a path across the blue and he strove to clear his mind.

4

AND ONE FOR OUR NEW FRIEND

Emma Geen

According to the Gospel of Matthew in the New Testament of the Christian Bible, when Jesus was just a few weeks old, the Angel of the Lord appeared to his father Joseph. He told him to take the child and Jesus' mother, Mary, down into Egypt to escape the massacre that King Herod, King of the Jews, had ordered when he had been told that a new king, the Messiah long foretold in Jewish tradition, had been born.

Whether or not such a massacre ever took place, the tradition that Jesus and his family fled to Egypt is as old as the Gospels which were written down some sixty to ninety years after his birth—between AD 60–90.

Central to the teaching of Jesus was the importance of care for the stranger, the outcast, the downtrodden and the poor. This reflects core Jewish teachings. However Jesus' own special development of this—reflected in the Lord's Prayer and in many of his stories and teachings, such as Matthew, 25: 31–46 (the story of the Sheep and the Goats, in which he says that on the Day of Judgement people will be divided as to whether they had helped the hungry, homeless and imprisoned, or ignored them) has a strong ring of personal experience. He taught that you should "love your enemy"; that you should welcome the stranger into your home; that you should protect the weak and vulnerable and should offer food to those who were without food.

In this interpretation Emma Geen has taken a story told within the tradition of the Coptic Church of Egypt about how and where the Holy Family lived while strangers in a foreign land. And she has created a story about what this taught the young Jesus, before he became a teacher himself. In doing so she gives a fascinating insight into what might well be the origin of some of Jesus' most powerful teachings about care for the stranger which has shaped Christian life ever since.

I t's nearly dark when the knock comes at the door. Mary hangs back as her husband answers, her fingers biting into the wood of the table. Yet as she listens her shoulders unknot. It's just a man that needs their help. They made a vow long ago and she finds herself glad to be fulfilling it now. She turns to scoop some of the leftover lentil stew into a bowl but is stopped by the sight of her eldest son standing in the bedroom doorway. Even fogged by sleep, his face is wide with concern. She kneels and takes his shoulders.

"There's nothing to be scared of. The man needs somewhere to stay a little while. He's lost his home."

His small brow pleats in concentration.

"You remember we told you how you were in exile when you were only a baby. Well there were some good people who helped us then and we must do the same."

As she brushes the hair from his forehead, she marvels, not for the first time, at the depth of his dark eyes. Though the face is unmistakably a child's, his look always strikes her as that of someone older than the sands. Fear strikes in her chest. Those eyes have seen everything from the heart of the sun to the depths of the earth. Is this humble house and frail body an exile as terrible as that of the man who came to their door? But her son is smiling, dimples belying his boyhood.

"I'm not scared."

She lets out a breath and kisses him on the brow, tasting the subtle notes of dust and sweat.

"Good." Whatever else he is, this boy is her son and this is his home. "Get to bed. We can talk further in the morning."

There is fire in the city. Cries of children, cut off, followed by piercing wails. He is held tight by his mother, father's back sliding ahead through the dark. Their old stable is lit a ghoulish orange but as he stares he sees that it is actually the archway of their current home. But now they are hurrying on, house dwindling to a spark behind them. He tries to reach out but his arms are swaddled tight, he is only a baby, nothing he can do. Then the shadows sweep them into their whirlpool of rushed footsteps and gasped breath, and their home is swallowed forever.

The rust red of dawn is creeping through the window when he wakes. His mouth is dry and muscles tight from the nightmare but it's not a real memory. He was too young to remember but the horror is all too easy to imagine. Though his parents delight in telling stories of their time in Egypt, questions about their escape are often answered only with the ashen complexion of their faces. He swallows the bad taste and sits, heart lightening as he remembers the events of yesterday evening. Is the man still there? He likes speaking to strangers, hearing their stories of other places and ways of living. Everyone has something interesting to say if you only listen. He skips over the prone forms of his brother and sister and dresses quickly. When he steps outside it's to find his mother already in the courtyard, hand around the grain scoop.

"Is he still here?"

She doesn't have to ask. "He's asleep in your father's workshop." She pours the grain into the saddle quern and drops the scoop back into the basket. "Don't disturb him, he must be exhausted."

The boy eyes the pile of barley, the same amount as they normally use. Are they not feeding the man?

His mother smiles, mistaking his hesitation. "He'll be awake soon enough and I'm sure he'll be happy to talk to you then but for now fetch me some water, please?"

He takes the pitcher from her with a nod and patters out into the street to follow the creep of the morning sun.

At the well, he climbs up the side and wedges his feet in a crack in the rocks to work the handle. The bucket has just winched up when he sees the sly shadow slinking around the edge of the courtyard. A fox. After chickens, no doubt. He cups his hands around his mouth and barks. The fox flees, the boy close after, whooping and small legs pounding the dust. He skids round the last house just in time to see

the orange streak into a small earth burrow. Too late. He kicks the sun-bleached shards of bones scattered around the entrance, then continues back to the well.

Bent by the weight of the water, his return home is more difficult but not so much so that he can resist the short detour past the workshop. Mother said to not disturb the stranger, but a peek can't hurt, can it? He places the pitcher down and leaps up and catches himself on the ledge with his elbows. It's dark inside, the gloom broken only with the sturdy shapes of the ploughs his father is building. The man can't have left already, can he? He leans in further, ignoring the ache of his arms as he peers, eyes strained as wide as the owl. Then he sees, there the stranger is, still asleep in the far corner, one of their hemp blankets drawn over a thin body. Isn't he hungry? Why was mother not making bread for him too? The man turns in his sleep and the boy startles backwards and lands flat in the dust. He scoops up the water and sprints round the corner, thoughts racing with his feet. How can it be that that fox has his hole but this man has nowhere to lay his head?

The grain has been ground to a fine flour by the time he steps into the courtyard and the full light of morning sun gleams in his mother's dark hair as she lowers the grinding stone to take the pitcher he offers.

He watches as she pours a splash of water in the dip she's made in the pile of flour, then swirls it into a loose mix and starts to knead. The sound of her work fills the morning quiet, a steady rhythm of dough slapping stone, the sigh of air being pushed from beneath it. Is that what it feels like to lose your home? To be plucked from a golden kernel and ground beyond recognition? The pale mix bulges away from

his mother's worn knuckles. Pushed from place to place? Never able to stop or rest?

His heart is heavy as he thinks of the man in their workshop and he lifts his eyes to his mother's face. "Does the man not get any bread?"

"Why do you say that?" Her gaze slips up from the work but she doesn't stop.

"You're using the same amount of flour as you always use."

"Ah." The sparkle returns to her eyes and the next thump of the dough is almost jubilant. "To answer that I shall have to tell you a story. You remember your father telling you how we crossed the border to Egypt?"

He nods.

"Well by then we were very tired and hungry. We headed for the closest town but we were turned away at every door. All through the neighbourhood we went, only begging for a little food or a place to stay the night but no one would help us even though servants that answered the door wore fine clothes and flocks of goats were stabled in their yards."

"Like when I was born."

"Yes, like that. And so we passed all the way through the town to the very outskirts where a small hovel sat with one haggard sheep tied outside. The door opened and we saw a—"

"The old woman." The boy pipes up, remembering the story.

His mother pushes a drop of sweat from her forehead with the back of a hand, one corner of her mouth lifting. "Yes, the old woman. By then I had all but given up hope. If the men in all those fine houses wouldn't help us, I thought, then surely one poor old woman wouldn't either. But she took one look at you nuzzled to my neck and opened the door wide. Inside she sat us down and gave us a drink and as we wet our parched throats she rummaged in a small box and came back beaming with a small loaf of bread and tiny roasted fish in her hands. I started to cry then, seeing she barely had enough to feed herself."

She pauses to throw some more flour upon the stone and the boy strains to pull himself level, as if he could reach to pluck the words like fruit.

"What then?"

"What then? Then she winked at me." His mother stretches the dough into a long snake between her hands, folding it in on itself and repeating as she enjoys his anticipation; but starting to knead once again, she continues. "She winked at me and, holding up the bread, tore it into three equal lumps. That done she took up a knife and cut the fish into three pieces, then put the bread and fish in a bowl and placed it on the table with the words: 'There. Now there are—'"

"Three fishes and three loaves of bread."

"Are you telling this or am I?" She frees one hand to make a lunge for his ribs. He ducks the tickle, giggling.

"It was a small miracle for your father and me to be shown such generosity when we needed it most. Yet she was the first of many good people to help us until your father had the dream telling us that we could return."

"But we didn't go back to Jerusalem."

"No, we heard that Herod's son had taken the throne and so we kept going north to your father's home. As we shut the door behind us on this house we remembered that kind old lady and vowed that we would help any stranger that came to it. And so we have."

After that the boy can't help feeling cheated, nor stop the tears rising behind his small voice. "But you're not making the man any bread."

She looks up sharply at the tone. "Am I not?" She tears off a lump from the dough and shapes it into a ball. "One for Jesus." She smiles at him and keeps plucking off handfuls. "One for Joseph. One for Mary. One for James. One for Hannah." The last is rolled towards him. "And one for our new friend."

He catches it, feeling the heat worked into the soft dough by his mother's hands. Following her example he pats it down into a disc and carries it over to the oven where Mary shows him how to toss the rounds onto the walls of the oven so that they will fall into the ashes when they are cooked. When it's done, they stand back together to admire the six rounds of bread stuck to the side, smaller than usual but good all the same.

"There." She dabs a spot of flour on his nose. "A small miracle."

PART TWO

HISTORICAL FOUNDATION

5

THOSE WHO WILL NEVER PASS THIS WAY AGAIN

Emma Geen

Daoism (sometimes spelt Taoism) is the oldest major religion of China. It is also the complete opposite of Confucianism, which with Buddhism is one of the other two major philosophical traditions of China. While Confucians were concerned with order and control based upon hierarchy and regulation, Daoists were free spirits who delighted in that which lies beyond order and which at times defies even what most would call belief.

At the heart of Daoism is a mysterious and beautiful book called the Dao de Jing (Tao Te Ching)—The Way and its Virtue. Dao is the Chinese word for path, road or way and for at least three thousand years it has also signified the Way of Heaven or the Way of Nature, encompassing the reality of what the cosmos is and how it works.

The author of this core book is known as Lao Zi, which simply means the Old Master, a term of respect given many years after his death. In life he was the chief historian of the archives of the small state of Chu and he lived in the 6th century BC. In his old age he despaired of the state of his kingdom and decided to go into exile beyond the borders of China as a protest at the corruption and abuses he saw all around him.

The main exit from ancient China was called the Gate to the West—a gap in the great Qinling Mountains of central China which stretch for over a hundred miles. It was here, according to legend, that the watchman on duty at this gateway to the outside world stopped the old man, a stranger, and asked him why he was leaving. Lao Zi told him and in response the gatekeeper asked him to write down his wisdom before he left so that the truth might remain accessible for those within China. Legend says he wrote the book in one night.

At the heart of it is the understanding that what we think we know is not what is true. This is captured in the famous opening line of Chapter One:

"The Dao (Way) that can be talked about is not the true Dao.
The name that can be named is not the eternal Name."

The book stresses time and time again, in a way that was unheard of at that time in China, that everyone and everything comes from a common source and is linked. No one and nothing is more important than anyone or anything else. From this has come the Daoist tradition of hospitality at all their temples and monasteries. And the belief, manifest in their actions, that all life is linked through the Dao.

China was not always this way.
At the west gate the guard has watched,
The back of peasants bow beneath the weight of work,
The back of officials bow beneath the weight of jewels,
And in every eye the gleam of gold,
Whilst above the heavens darken.

Day in, day out,
The crowds wash round him,
Until he knows every bearing,
Every step,
And even with eyes shut can separate,
The soldier's bloodied sweat,
The peasant's wearied stumble,
The merchant's calloused heels.

He knows which men will return within the day,
And those who will never pass again.

And so he watches with interest,
An old man atop a water buffalo.
A farmer, headed for the paddies,
But whose head bows over the beast's neck,
Like one who leaves forever.

Beneath the farmer's hat,
Peek long ear lobes,
A beard of white.
For despite rough clothing,
The man carries jade inside.
Lao Zi.
Keeper of the Archives.

The gatekeeper acts without thinking,
Flings himself round the buffalo's neck.
"Don't rob us your wisdom,
Not without a remembrance,
A record."

Lao Zi regards the gatekeeper,
Eyes clear grey,
But says nothing.
Does nothing.
Then, at last, dismounts.
Seated on the garrison floor,
He is as still as the river bed,
Whilst the gatekeeper rushes back and forth,
Fetching parchment, ink, brush,
Candles, food, drink.

Only when dust settles,
Does a thin wrist unfurl,
Long fingers,
Brush balanced,
Repose so refined,
That it seems,
It is the parchment that moves.

The gatekeeper watches,
Wide eyes glistening,
With the dance of candle flame and characters,
Clothed in velvet black.

Chang, a steady tempo.
Kei, whipping up a melody.
Fei, countering every step.
And at the vortex's centre,
Dao.

Stroke after stroke,

Uncertain world orbits,
Until gatekeeper has to step outside.
Hand resting on the buffalo's haunch,
Breathing in its mossy sweet,
He watches the sun sink,
As light leaves the fetid kingdom.

Dawn creeps in stillborn blue,
To the rasp of brush,
That slows,
Pauses,
Stops.

The gatekeeper startles awakes,
Stares at the bundle held towards him.

And so the Old Master passes,
From the gate,
From knowledge,
From history,
Leaving nothing,
But five thousand characters,
Clutched to the gatekeeper's chest.

As the buffalo dwindles,
He looks at the elegant swirls of ink,
Lips moving silently,
Where the Dao De Jing begins.

DAO called DAO is not the real DAO.

6

NOT FOR A
MOUNTAIN OF GOLD

Jumana Moon

When the Prophet Mohammed first started preaching in the early 7th century that there was One God, he did so in perhaps the most danger-ous place he could find. His home city, the city of Makkah in Arabia, was the centre of a vast cult of pagan deities and rituals focused upon the mysterious black stone built into the walls of the Kaba. Pilgrims from across Arabia and beyond came on pilgrimage to worship the many deities in the sanctuary around the Kaba and the city merchants and people made their fortunes from the pilgrims.

Therefore when in around AD 622 Mohammed started to preach that these deities were false gods and that there was just One God, Allah, he brought down upon himself and his first followers the wrath of the city. Mohammed advised his followers that they should seek refuge from the persecution by going to Christian places of sanctuary. Some went to the monastery of Saint Catherine on Mount Sinai in the Egyptian desert and were given sanctuary there. The largest group took ship to the Christian kingdom of Abyssinia, now Ethiopia, and asked the king to give them refuge. What happened next is the subject of this story and is based upon Islamic teachings and stories whose authenticity has been ensured by Islamic tradition.

Often when people hear about the hijra or emigration of the early Muslims they think of when Prophet Mohammed (pbuh)[1] and the new Muslim community left Makkah for Medina. This hijra to Medina marks the beginning of the Islamic calendar and is a very significant event in Islamic history. However there was an earlier hijra, the first hijra, and this is the story of what happened…

Bismillah arahman araheem
With the name of God, All Compassionate, All Merciful

This is a story from the early days of Islam, from the days of Prophet Mohammed, upon him be peace, when the new Muslim community was very small. You may have heard something of the clan of the Quraish, a powerful, rich clan who ruled and controlled Makkah and the surrounding areas. The Quraish were not pleased with the new ideas the Prophet (pbuh) spoke about and taught—they did not like the challenge to their power or the threat to their control over the city. So, as with many powerful people when they fear that they may lose their power, the Quraish began to pursue and persecute those early Muslims. At first it was name-calling, excluding them, hurling abuse at them—bullying really. Then gradually this increased to throwing rubbish and stones at them, until people were injured. It was not long after that some Muslims were killed by the Quraish and the risks to the new Muslims were very grave, particularly for those who were not from well-known or well-connected families and so had little protection.

Mohammed (pbuh) knew that these people needed safety, it was too dangerous for them to stay in Makkah. He also knew that across the Red Sea, in Abyssinia, there lived a king with a great reputation for being just and wise. He was a Christian king, whom the people called *al Najashi*—the Negus. So the decision was made to send the most vulnerable Muslims to Abyssinia, to the Negus, to seek asylum.

This small group, comprised of men, women and children, slipped away from Makkah under the cover of night, for fear of being seen. They travelled by foot, heading west across the desert, towards the coast and they made good progress. But when the Quraish discovered they were gone, they set off after them, riding fine, fast Arabian horses whose hooves almost flew over the ground, muscles and manes rippling and with such speed that the men of the Quraish easily began to catch up with the fleeing Muslims. The Muslims heard the horses and the men approaching and looked around for somewhere to hide. Seeing a large sand dune they crouched down behind it, though as they looked back they saw to their horror that they had left a trail of footprints that led right to their hiding place.

So the people cupped their upturned hands in prayer and they prayed for protection and as they did so the desert winds lifted and the desert sands shifted and swirled and then settled—right into their fresh footprints, completely covering their tracks. The Quraish lost the trail and had no choice but to return back to Makkah.

The Muslims pressed on, always to the west, until finally they reached the Red Sea port of Shu'ayba where they boarded a boat bound for Abyssinia. And I wonder how it was for them as they stood on the deck and watched their homeland grow smaller and more distant as the boat sailed away from the shore. And I wonder what each one of them thought about: perhaps they thought of the people they loved and feared they would not see again; the places where they had been happy that they would not return to; sounds and smells of their country which they may now only have the memories of; the tastes of food they had grown up with; the taste of home.

Soon the boat had pulled far out to sea and Shu'ayba and the Arabian shore faded out of sight and a new shore, the coast of Abyssinia, came into view from the west. Once they had landed the Muslims were received by the court of the Negus and were given what they needed and made very welcome.

For a little while all was well, until the Quraish heard that the Muslims were in Abyssinia and sent two emissaries with gifts of gold for the king, to convince him to send the refugees back to Makkah. The Negus, never one to rush into a decision, said that he could not send the Muslims back without hearing from them and so a man named Ja'far spoke and explained something of the new religion to the Negus and the court. He spoke of the teachings of caring for the needy, fairness, respect and kindness in dealings with others. He spoke of the teachings of offering regular prayers and observing fasting, of the teaching of belief in the Unity of God. When the Negus asked him about the Qur'an, Ja'far recited part of Surat Maryam, the Chapter of Mary, and how it tells of the miraculous birth of her son 'Isa, Jesus (upon him be peace). He spoke so beautifully, with such devotion and such clarity that the Negus and his bishops wept until the tears rolled down their faces. "These words and the words of Jesus are as rays of light radiating from the same source," exclaimed the Negus. He continued to say that he would not allow the emissaries of the Quraish to take the Muslims back to Makkah.

Displeased with this the men told the Negus that the Muslims spoke badly of Jesus, insulting him. The Negus, troubled, called Ja'far back to him and asked him to explain this. Ja'far spoke once again, saying that Jesus, or 'Isa in Arabic, was regarded as a Messenger of God, His Prophet, and was much respected and esteemed in Islam—there was nothing but love felt by the Muslims for 'Isa, upon him be peace.

At this the Negus took his sceptre and drew a thin, straight line on the earth floor of his court. He then raised the sceptre from the ground and declared to the whole court: "There is nothing more than this line between our two religions. Not for a mountain of gold will I send these people back to Makkah."

Taking all the gold and gifts they had come with, but no refugees, the men of the Quraish returned to Makkah. The Muslims lived on in Abyssinia and found under the protection of the Negus the security, peace and tranquillity they sought. The Muslims lived side by side with their Abyssinian neighbours; lived as the loyal and contented subjects of a wise and just king and his most hospitable people.

1 Muslims use (pbuh)—peace be upon him—as a prayer and blessing after the name of Prophet Mohammed. We also make the prayer for peace after the names of all the other prophets of the Bible, e.g. Adam, Noah, Jonah, etc. (peace be upon them all).

7

MANY, MANY MOONS

Benaifer Bhandari

Zoroastrianism is the ancient traditional religion of Persia. Its name comes from the Prophet Zarathustra whose name was converted by Greek writers into Zoroaster. It is not certain when Zarathustra lived. It was possibly as early as the 12th century BC or more likely in the 6th century BC.

In the 7th century AD Persia was invaded by the Arabs and Islam became the ruling faith even though the vast majority of the people remained either Zoroastrians or Christians.

By the 10th century waves of persecution had worn down followers of both religions, but especially the Zoroastrians. While the Qur'an speaks of the Jews and Christians as fellow People of the Book and thus offers them some degree of protection (as in the previous story, too), the Zoroastrians were seen by many Muslims as pagans who believed in many gods rather than in One God. This meant life was very difficult for them especially in periods of particular fanaticism which from time to time arose in Persia.

This is why in the 10th century a major group of Zoroastrians fled from Persia and went into exile. Their wandering eventually brought them to the west coast of India. And here, after their initial landing was questioned, they were given refuge and a welcome—as this story tells.

Today the descendants of the Zoroastrians still live on the west coast of India, especially in the city of Mumbai. They are known as the Parsees—from the word "Persians". Built into their temple and community life is generosity to those who are not Zoroastrians and especially to outcasts and to strangers.

This story tells us why.

I am so scared.

Father told me tales as I was growing up, of traders coming to these parts and then returning home several shades darker of skin because the sun chose to shine so fiercely on this part of the world. Yet our ship is being blown about by a wind so dark and strong in power it doesn't allow me a single glimpse of the sun to warm my bones.

My journey began years ago when I was a girl, under cover of darkness, full of fear. I was surprised that those who hunted us did not smell our terror. Father meticulously planned our escape. He led me to the sea and entrusted *Ava Mehr*, the sea's guardian, to carry us away on her waves from the horrors we faced in our beloved Iran to a land where we could be free to worship all the good creations of *Ahura Mazda* in peace and amongst tolerance. I decided, right then, that wheresoever *Ava Mehr* took us would be as equally beloved as Iran, if not more. Sanctuary is worth adoring.

"It may take many, many moons" Father had said and I had nodded hopefully.

The cold, however, has robbed me of all hope and fear settles in again. I see it in the eyes of the others too. The

water rages around us, waves reaching higher than twenty of the tallest men, first over one side of our ship then the other.

My uncle, our head priest, is looking around at desolate faces and now stands up, tall, with legs slightly apart so the wind can't push him over.

"Brothers and sisters, hear me. Do not fear, do not forget!" he says. "Let us protect ourselves, let us pray."

And all together, with one voice, we pray:

"Ashem Vohu
Vahishtem Asti
Ushta Asti Ushta Ahmai
Hyat Ashai Vahishtai
Ashem!"

Even before we finish, I look around and babies have settled in their mothers' arms, children are closing their eyes to sleep. Wondrously, *Ava Mehr*'s waters now only reaches the height of five men, then two and then, finally, stillness.

I cannot allow sleep to overtake me like it has everyone else, but I can breathe deep breaths and, like Uncle said, try not to forget. When Father realised there was not enough space for him on our voyage, his gifts to me were two ancient mantras, *Ashem Vohu* to use as my shield and *Yatha Ahu Vairyo* as my spear. Remembering, I do not feel so cold.

My meditation is interrupted by a cry from a child who obviously cannot sleep either. A tremor, an excitement, works its way towards me as we see what the child sees. Land. With the mantra still ringing in our ears and hanging in the air around us, this sight fills us all with unbelievable hope.

With joy on their faces, all the men help to guide our ship towards land. We women begin to gather our few belongings and our children, our eyes twinkling and hearts daring to soar.

Now I believe it—*Spenta Armaiti*, our adored Mother Earth! As we step onto her, like everyone else I bend down and gather a handful of her, pressing her against my forehead and my chest. Untying my *kusti* from around my waist I begin to pray, to all the guardian spirits, in all four directions, with deep gratitude in my heart. So lost am I in this moment that I only just notice Uncle, in wordless communication with a man from these parts who is clearly a guard and clearly not happy.

Finishing my prayers quickly I rush over and ask Uncle

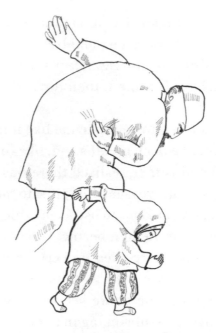

if I may help. By the age of five I could speak five languages and each year I added one more until my tenth year. Father taught me the world is very big and it is also very small and so he filled my childhood with the language and the colour of all the places he had been to and all the people he had heard of.

With a nod from Uncle I hesitantly try to connect some of the languages that Father collected, with the height and colour and style of dress of the guard before me. I think I see the corner of the guard's mouth twitch as I hit upon familiar words, so using that language I translate what Uncle is saying, translating back a simple statement: "You will attend court now and explain yourselves."

My joy now is tempered with a little hesitation as Uncle gathers his fellow priests and we follow the guard. We have…no…we had, many palaces in our beloved Iran, but none looked like this one. I wish we were wearing finer clothes but decide that for today the goodness in our hearts will be the only finery we bring.

My philosophising comes to an abrupt stop as we enter the court. The splendour threatens to overwhelm me but Uncle sees and gently whispers: "Just do as I do." Walking forwards, past the guard who stays at the entrance, we make our way into the centre of this lavish space.

From a raised platform we are being watched by a lady and a man, majestically dressed and sitting tall in the way that only those who feel safe can sit. Uncle stops before them and bows low. In my eagerness I bow even lower. Not having bowed in all my years, I want to do it properly as I am keen to make a good impression. "Be yourself," whispers Uncle, having caught the extra flourish of my arms as I struggle to keep my balance and bring myself back upright.

The lady looks kind but it is the man who speaks. "I am Jadev Rana, ruler of this land. Who are you and why are you here?"

I whisper the translation and Uncle takes a deep breath. "Great King, we are poor strangers and have come to you for protection. Having fled our home to save our religion the waters have brought us here, to you. We crave sanctuary and you have compassionate eyes, sire."

I look around and the courtiers are looking upon us thoughtfully. The Queen in particular seems to have been touched by Uncle's words. Jadav Rana, however, looks less certain.

"My land," says he, leaning backwards as if the conversation is over, "is full." My heart tightens at these words but I try to focus on Uncle who asks me to tell the guard to bring in two bowls. One filled full of milk and one with sugar.

Uneasiness spreads through the room at Jadav Rana's last words and Uncle's strange request. Only the Queen keeps calm, looking with gentleness at Uncle and at me. The minute that it takes for the two bowls to arrive feels like a lifetime to me—somehow I know that whatever happens next will determine my future and those of my children. I breathe deeply as Father taught me to and watch in amazement.

Without words Uncle points to the bowl of milk and then gestures the whole room. Ah, I think he means the milk represents Jadav Rana and his people. Uncle then points to the sugar, gesturing our little group. Then slowly Uncle begins to pray "*Yatha Ahu Vairyo…*" and it all begins to make sense as Uncle steadily pours the whole bowl of sugar into the already full bowl of milk.

Uncle's face glows. "The milk, it does not spill. Instead it is sweetened!" This does not need translating as every person in the court appreciates what they have just witnessed. I feel a release in my heart as most importantly, all uncertainty has left the eyes of Jadav Rana.

He nods and says: "You are indeed a wise man to have persuaded me without words. You will have my consent…as soon as I have yours."

Uncle is quick to say: "O wise ruler, we are ready to consent. Just say to what."

Jadav Rana contemplates what to say next but I can tell from his manner that he feels that what he is about to ask for is a little extreme—if only he knew how desperate we are for refuge.

"Very well." And Jadav Rana begins his list. "First,

explain your religion to me. My lookouts have watched you and your people praying on the beach and your actions seem so similar to ours but I have to know more. Second, to prop-erly share our land you must share our language, so please give yours up and speak only ours. Third, to integrate truly, you must adopt our dress so our people and your people begin to have much in common. Fourth, for our mutual peace you must lay aside your arms and promise never to use them, and lastly, so we can attend your contracts, your marriage ceremonies must be carried out in the evening."

The last condition the King required amuses us a little as we have the custom of joining ourselves in marriage precisely at the time the sun joins the moon, so this is definitely the easiest promise to make.

I have never been as proud of Uncle as I am at this moment. He begins by explaining our beautiful religion, our passion for all the elements that *Ahura Mazda* has created, our prayers, our *kusti* around our waist and all the many rituals we have in adoration of the goodness around us. Jadav Rana looks pleased as Uncle says: "You will be given no reason to doubt us, o generous King. We promise to make this our home and protect this land and all in it, for always."

With thoughts of my future exciting my mind I do not even notice the beautiful Queen—she is standing right next to me with open arms. With a quick glance at Uncle, who gives me a little nod, I accept the Queen's embrace. All my life I have wondered what my Mother's embrace would feel like. I still do not know for sure, but for the first time in many, many moons I feel warm and I feel safe.

8

FEASTING BY FAITH

Told by Reverend Eustace Kabue
Written by Emma Geen

*It is impossible to date the great stories of African traditional belief as
they are truly timeless in their content. This story comes from Nairobi
in 2012 where the* Stories of the Stranger *team hosted an evening of
stories told by Christian, Hindu and Muslim African leaders. Today
many such stories form part not just of traditional African beliefs but
also shape and inform African Christian and Muslim traditions.
Certainly throughout Africa there are models of hospitality and of care
for the stranger. In the huge upheavals that Africa has experienced in
the last twenty to thirty years, the scale of refugees pouring into countries such as Kenya has been in the millions. The need therefore to
preserve the African tradition of hospitality so wonderfully described
here could not be more important.*

The Kikuyu community are from around Mount
Kenya in the East African highlands and they
believe that the God who created them lives on the
height of the mountain. He's the almighty God, the creator,

high and mighty like the mountains. He's the creator of the mountains and he's also gracious and generous—he gives water, he is the light. We call him "the God of *kirinyaga*", which is the equivalent of "light" in Kikuyu. So he's the God of light, the giver of life, the giver of plenty because from the mountains you have the rivers that flow to the rest of the country, so the land is rich and wealthy with forests, rainforests, wildlife, good farmland. So the land is very productive.

But it's not so with the neighbours to the East and one day one of those ladies, Mwende, was left behind when, during times of drought, her husband went off to look for food from some neighbouring communities, never to return. So she was alone to fend for herself and her son Mutua.

And they used to remember some neighbours who used to have cows. There was some flour that was left and they wanted to prepare an African cake made from maize flour— we call it *ugali*. It's a bit tough if there's no soup, water, milk or tea to go with it, or some vegetables. But in these times the cows had died off from drought and famine so they didn't even have milk to prepare the little remaining flour that she had to feed herself and the baby. So, in order that they would be able to feed on the dry, hard African cake made from the remaining flour, she would tell the little boy stories about the milk that they could have got from the neighbour's cow in better days.

"Form that cake in some kind of container and then dip it in the milk of the neighbour's cow and eat it quickly before the milk spills," she would tell him. Of course the milk was imaginary—it was just supposed to help the child

eat that dry African cake. He was feasting on the dry cake by faith because there was nothing else to survive on. So faith worked, but even that ran out and they had nothing to eat.

They had to move on, out of the village, and go to the neighbouring community. They travelled to Kikuyuland and, fortunately for them, the Kikuyu have a tradition of constructing shelters along the pathways for travellers and providing food, porridge, sugar cane, sweet potatoes, arrowroots, roasted bananas, roasted maize and sour milk and water so that travellers are able to eat. They believe that it is a curse if someone dies of hunger within their neighbourhood if they could have provided for them—be it a stranger, a visitor, or a relative.

So they were able to find shelter on their journey but

they wanted to get to a village where they would find people, accommodation and rest.

Eventually they arrived at the home of Wambui and her husband Mwangi. Again, the Kikuyu have a tradition that when a visitor comes he or she is welcomed and given something to eat. Then the visitor is asked about news. Those were the days when there were no newspapers, no radios, no mobile phones. The means of communication was largely by word of mouth. Travellers would bring accounts about the weather conditions, about circum-stances of peace, or about warfare. They would bring new information, and so were an important source of communi-cation between communities.

And here they were received warmly.

Wambui and Mwangi didn't know if this woman, Mwende, and her son, Mutua, were friends or enemies, but they knew it is better to treat strangers kindly because you don't know what may end up happening. And they also had a Kikuyu tradition whereby poor people are received into the family and are allowed a certain portion of land. When they harvested their crops they left some for wild animals, for birds in the wilderness, and for poor people. So Mwende and Mutua were easily accommodated into the family and given a patch for harvesting. And gradually they adapted to this family and over time Mwende became a second wife to Mwangi and part of the wider family. It was a kind of polyg-amous situation, which was good because her original husband had disappeared never to be seen again. And now with another husband she was looked after.

It is said that out of the ten clans of the Kikuyu commu-nity two have come from Ukambani, the place where

Mwende came from. And one of these two clans is considered to have become one of the two royal ruling classes. This clan is called the Acera. The Acera clan is also considered to be among the wise people, the ones that helped to make decisions in the council of elders.

I can tell you that I'm standing here myself as a descendant of the Acera clan. The Bible is very clear about receiving strangers into your own family: receive strangers, be hospitable to strangers, because you may never know but you may be receiving angels. Maybe I'm here because Mwende was received from Ukambani to Kikuyuland and became part of that Acera clan of which I'm a descendant.

9

THE END OF THE WORLD

Emma Geen

The Baha'i¹ faith is the most recent of the main world religions. It arose in Islamic Persia and its roots are firmly within the Islamic tradition though it has now become a world religion in its own right. Its founder, Baha'u'llah, declared in 1863 that he was the new Prophet, in the line of prophets from Krishna, Buddha, Zoroaster, Abraham, Moses, Jesus and Mohammed. In the 1840s a teacher called The Bab, meaning the Gate, had predicted the coming of a new prophet and had been murdered. This claim, that Mohammed was not the last of the Prophets sent to reveal the Words of God and His Will, aroused massive opposition in Persia and brought persecution down upon the original followers of Baha'u'llah.

In response to his teachings the Persian authorities first of all imprisoned him and then sent him into exile. They sent him to a prison cell in the most remote, barren and backward part of the Ottoman Empire: the city of Akka in Palestine, the Holy Land for Jews and Christians. Here he continued to preach and to receive pilgrim visitors even while he was in jail. As this story tells, in the second half of the 19th century Akka was considered the back of beyond. Yet it was here that Baha'u'llah's message of world unity and peace began to spread around the world, even touching the hearts of his jailers whose attitude towards this exiled stranger changed dramatically when they heard him speak.

Today it is possible to visit the house to which Baha'u'llah was released and where he died in 1892, aged seventy-four. It lies between the cities of Acre (modern day Akka) and Haifa where the body of The Bab is buried.

There are some that call Akka the end of the world. I've always called it home myself, but on the days when the sun is a molten core in the humid sky I can near understand why. It sure isn't pretty here, there's no arguing against that. The main city is a twisted honeycomb of streets and crumbling houses that loom like dour sentinels, all caked with enough mud and crap and damp to set the flies and fleas dancing for joy. Some even say that the air here is so foul that birds fall dead from the sky. People like to exaggerate, see. I've only ever seen one bird fall myself. Well two, but the second was so riddled with maggots that I'm surprised he'd gotten airborne in the first place. Yet whatever is said about Akka, you have to understand that a man's home is his home, whether it's perched on the world's brink or not.

The infamy of Akka is helped none by the fact that for many of the folk here it isn't home, what with our prison complex. This is the trade Akka supplies, see, we take out the empire's trash and lock them up under bolt and key. You name it we've got it, the worst murderers, arsonists, robbers, political dissidents, thugs that'd rather take your eye out than give you the time of day. To see all of them put out of harm's way is almost satisfying if you like that sort of thing and, seeing guarding is in my blood, I guess it is for me. So the rare time when we get thrown a lot that don't really belong here I can smell them a mile off.

It was like that with that old fella and his group—Mirza Husayn-Ali Nuri, though that wasn't what his folks called him. We'd been told that they were enemies of the state so there was a large crowd gathered to jeer from the harbour. Yet after the eight hours crossing, getting off that ship, they looked less like enemies and more like mezze that had been left too long on the fire.

Over the coming weeks, my doubts were only to grow. We weren't allowed to talk with the prisoners but you don't need words to tell the mark of a man. Merely walk past the cells of some here and they'll launch at the bars, frothing with expletives that would turn most men crimson. And don't get me started on the shit-flingers. But that old religious man, he was the exact opposite. Pass his cell and at most he'd look up to give you a polite nod, then keep on writing. Throw him to the ground and he'd rise as dignified as if he'd just been in prayer. Later, when we'd stopped roughing him around so much he'd even smile and thank you when you brought him his meal. Whenever I saw that smile I'd get the strangest feeling that he belonged in some quiet house in the country, surrounded by his grandchildren, not locked up here in some damp cell.

His eldest son was another one like him. Abdu'l-Baha was what they called him and he was always looking after someone or other. A lot of people get sick in the prison, what with the dirt and heat, yet even when he was so taken with the fever that he could barely sit straight he'd still be

looking after his people. Acted more like a saint than a criminal, he did.

I wasn't the only one that thought there was something different about that lot. It wasn't long after they arrived when we started getting people turning up at the city gate proclaiming themselves pilgrims of all things. Stubborn ones at that. Most of the trash we get sent here are the sort people are glad to be rid of and if they do send anything after it's a well-aimed spit. So naturally, I was curious, especially when I'd been turning one young man away for more than a month.

"So what is it about this old man?" I said as I tugged him up from his spot one day.

"*His name* is Baha'u'llah." He said as he wriggled from my grip, all flame in his eyes.

Baha'u'llah! Now, call me cynical, but it's hardly surprising that someone who goes around calling himself "Glory of God" got himself locked up. I'd long since stopped counting how many we've in our cells who claim to be some relation or other of God's; yet I'd never taken Mirza for a crazy like that. So instead of moving this boy along, I questioned him further.

He told me that the people we had locked up next to the barracks were Baha'is: a new religion that had sprung from that Bab figure who caused all that uproar a couple of decades back. The Baha'is, he said, believe that religious history shows itself through a series of divine messengers who start religions suited to the needs of their time, including Moses, Buddha, Jesus and Mohammed, but hear this: the most recent was supposed to be none other than old Mirza!

The bit that really made me pause though was when he said that Mirza had been in exile for nearly twenty years. When I thought of how long that man had been pushed from place to place it filled me with a horrid feeling, like maggots squirming about my insides.

As I listened, you could see the hope spreading across this man's face. Sure I was intrigued, even a little touched, but it doesn't pay to let the other guards see you getting too friendly with the pilgrims and so as soon as I heard the march of the approaching patrol, I hoofed this boy on his way. Besides, I knew he'd be straight back the next day.

Sometimes the pilgrims even brought food and drink for this "Baha'u'llah". We ate well in the barracks those nights. But even the best of breads tasted stale when I let my thoughts rove to that old man in his cell—the only bread the prisoners get is black and salty as a sailor's beard. So whenever this happened I got in the habit of taking the old man a bit. That way we got to talking. I wasn't the only guard he'd charmed by then and so the restrictions had been relaxed. Mostly we'd talk about what he'd been writing that day; he sent letters to fancy folk you wouldn't believe—the Pope, Alexander of Russia, Queen Victoria. I could only shake my head in awe but he'd just smile.

"Humankind is a unity," he'd always say. "The need of the present time is to establish global unity." And his eyes would be as clear and glorious as the morning sun.

Pretty soon, it didn't seem so crazy that those pilgrims travelled all this way just to catch a glimpse of him.

When I get to thinking of those conversations, I start wondering what would have happened if they'd gone on for longer. He had a way about him of turning men's hearts. But it was only a couple of months after that his youngest son fell through a skylight. Pierced right through his ribs. Not a quick or pleasant death by anyone's standards. Soon after, the Baha'is were moved into better accommodation. Last I heard, that old man was shacked up in some empty mansion outside the city. Good for him, I say.

Still, every time I pass his old cell I smile to see the spot by the window where he'd sit scribbling and I get to thinking—What if that old fella really is a prophet? What if these

Baha'is are the religion of the new age? For if Akka is the end of this world, then I suppose it's also got to be the beginning of the next.

<hr />

[1] In the interests of accessibility the diacritics have been dropped from certain names in this story. The traditional spelling of these names is as follows: Abdu'l-Bahá, Bahá'i, Bahá'u'lláh and Mírzá Husayn-'Alí Núrí.

PART THREE

FOLK

10

OH, IT'S SO GOOD TO SEE YOU

Anna Conomos

Martin was a Roman soldier who in the early 4th century became fascinated by the strange new religion of Christianity. He was slow to convert fully, because he soon realised that becoming a Christian would challenge his professional life as a soldier—at this time, Christianity taught that no one should show violence to another person and banned Christians from joining the army.

After the dramatic twenty-four hours of his conversion, which is told in this story, Martin went on to found the first monastic order in the West and to this day he is remembered as a great saint, monk and teacher. His name comes from the word Mars, the Roman god of War, from which we also get the word "martial arts". And this truly is a story of the transformation of the hard warrior into somebody more important and memorable, through his care for a stranger.

The Western monastic tradition was founded in the 6th century by Saint Benedict, who was profoundly influenced by Saint Martin. It has the tradition that every visitor who turns up at the monastery should be viewed as being Christ and that nobody should ever be turned away empty handed or refused at least a night's rest and safety.

The old beggar sunk to his knees, certain that this would be his last night. Icy winds had left him numb: he had no feeling left in any of his limbs; his eye-lids were heavy with exhaustion and his half-naked, shivering body had turned blue from the bitter cold. Around him passers-by watched the poor, miserable heap with disgust.

"Move out of the way!"

"Oh, Mummy! What *is* that?"

The man closed his eyes and fell forwards. All at once, he felt a hand, someone's arm lifting him up. It was a soldier! With a sword! And a beautiful Roman military coat! The coat was bright red and made of the warmest wool; it had a shimmering gold brooch encrusted with jewels fastened around the neck.

The soldier drew his sword; he held it high up in the air. The beggar winced as he watched the sword being brought down with force, but instead of chopping off his head, the soldier chopped clean through his beautiful red coat! And then, stranger still, he picked up one half of the coat (the better half) and placed it over the beggar's head and shoulders, fastening it carefully around him with the gold clasp, while he took the remaining piece of fabric and threw it over his own bare shoulders. The young man then placed his sword back in his belt, smiled at the poor man, frowned at the shame-faced crowd that had gathered and walked on.

Who was he? Where had he come from? Where was he going? Well, I'll tell you his story.

His name was Martin, a name given to him by his father because it means "warrior". His father was a Roman officer and his greatest dream was that his son would follow in his

carefully laid out footsteps and also become an esteemed member of the Roman military. But Martin had a very different dream, a secret dream that he did not dare reveal to his pagan parents. As a young child, Martin had once overheard a bishop telling wonderful stories about a holy man called Jesus Christ who showed love to everyone, especially to the poor, the sick and the needy. Jesus worked miracles and taught people to be kind and peace-loving.

Since that day, Martin had felt a burning desire to follow his example and be baptised as a Christian. His parents, as you can imagine, had other plans. When Martin reached the tender age of fifteen, he was sent to Amiens, in Gaul, to join the army of Emperor Julian. Aloft on his noble steed and clad in a beautiful red coat Martin sallied forth one very cold and windy night.

This is exactly where we met him at the start of this story when he shared his coat with the dying beggar. He had to admit that half his body nearly froze solid through exposure to the treacherously cold wind. It was with a grateful heart that he sank beneath his bedclothes when he finally reached the soldiers' camp. There, as he lay, his thoughts turned to the beggar whom he had left on the icy streets, and he felt very guilty. He didn't even know the poor man's name…but then sleep overtook him. All of a sudden, Martin became aware of a bright light next to his bed; he opened his eyes and saw the strangest sight: it was a man, right there in front of him, wearing a very familiar red cloak around his shoulders fastened with a golden clasp!

"Oh, it's so good to see you," Martin began. "Are you all right?"

"Martin, you have performed a great deed of love for me. I was cold and you gave me half your cloak."

"How do you know my name? Who are you?"

"I am Jesus Christ."

"I thought you were a…wait!" But the man had already disappeared and the tent was once more plunged into darkness. And then Martin remembered Christ's words from the Bible: "Whatever you do to the poorest of your brothers, you do to me."

Of course after his vision Martin could not sleep a wink. He could still feel inside him the delicious warmth from the radiant light of Christ. Before the break of dawn he crept out of the campsite and, still wrapped in only half a cloak, he found his way to the nearest church. Rousing the priest, he insisted on being baptised that very day, that very minute in fact. From then on, he longed to serve Christ in every way possible.

Not long after Martin's baptism, a barbarian army invaded Gaul and every soldier had to appear before the Emperor to receive arms in order to fight off the intruding army. "How could I lift a finger against any human creature?" thought Martin. "But then how can I avoid doing so?"

Just as his turn came to be called up, he stood before all of his comrades, hundreds of them. He took a deep breath and turned to the Emperor Julian.

"I can't do it!" His voice echoed in the silent courtyard.

"I beg your pardon?"

"I...I can't fight for you anymore. I have served you as a soldier these past five years, now let me serve Christ. Give these weapons to those who are prepared to fight; they are wasted on me."

Everyone began to roar with laughter. "You coward!" they shouted,

"You're just scared!"

"Soldier for Christ, eh? You only want to see us all killed and save your own face."

Martin felt himself going red. His resolve was weakening, but then he remembered the beggar in the street who had been scorned by all the passers-by and the vision of Christ by his bedside, bathed in light. He took another deep breath and cried, "That's not true, and I'll prove it to you. Tomorrow I'll stand in the front line of battle, completely unarmed except in the armour of Christ."

Silence. The Emperor pursed his lips.

"Quite the hero then. Well, since you seem so keen to sacrifice yourself, why should we stand in your way? So be it! Lock him up!"

And Martin was carried off to be held in a cell where he would spend the night before being taken to the battlefield on the following day.

But by some miracle, the very next morning, the barbarian army regretted its action and asked for peace! So there was no war and Martin had to be released—much to the disappointment of some of his colleagues who had been looking forward to a touch of blood. Martin, now free, went straight to the Bishop who wasted no time and promptly made him a deacon. Martin longed for a quiet and secluded life away from the hustle and bustle of busy crowds and noisy streets, so he decided to build a small monastery for himself, the first monastery ever to be founded in Gaul...but he was not left alone for long. Word began to spread that there was a Christian monk who healed lepers, who could revive those on the brink of death, who could perform miracles.

People came from far and wide to seek his help and Martin turned no-one away. In fact, on one occasion, a certain man was brought to him by villagers nearby. This man was red in the face, his hair dishevelled, his clothes torn, his eyes wild and frantic.

The villagers dragged him to Martin crying out, "They said you can help, we had no one else to turn to, the man is mad; be careful, he bites." The madman gnashed his teeth at Martin but the latter looked at him kindly, stroked his hair,

spoke to him and then pronounced healing on him in the name of Christ. From that day on, the madman never bared his teeth again.

In time, the Bishop of the great town of Tours died. Martin had, of course, become so popular that everyone wanted him to be the new Bishop. So they went to find him, but he was nowhere to be seen; he had heard the rumours and had run off to find a hiding place. But people every-where knew him. In desperation Martin spied some geese in a nearby shed and ran inside to hide. The geese, in turn, got the shock of their lives and began to cackle and hiss and run in all directions flapping their wings. They caused such a commotion that they of course betrayed Martin's awkward hiding place immediately and so, resigning himself to God's will, Martin allowed himself to be taken to Tours and be ordained Bishop.

He proceeded to build a new monastery just outside the town and, despite his new position, he insisted on living humbly and simply, making sure that the buildings were spacious enough to accommodate any passer-by. Thanks to Martin's shining example and missionary activity, eighty monks joined his new community in no time at all and his fame spread day by day, even reaching the ears of high ranking officials and governors of the empire.

One day the Emperor himself invited Martin to feast with him in his own home. That very same day, Martin had passed by the prison in Tours and remembered his own time behind bars as a young man so many years earlier. He pitied the prisoners who begged for help and when he presented himself before the Emperor he had an unusual request—but this time he felt no fear, no hesitation: "Your Excellency, I shall not sit down to feast with you before you have granted me one wish: that you free the innocent men who are suffering in your prison in Tours." Impressed by his courage, the Emperor ordered that they be released immediately and from that day on he became a great supporter of Martin's work and his monastic community.

Years passed, and at the ripe old age of eighty Martin gathered his monks around him and warned them that he would not be with them for much longer. He finally reposed on the eighth of November, 397.

His popularity has survived over the centuries to this very day: pilgrimages to Tours, churches named in his honour and crosses with sculpted images of his life and story. People the world over have been named after him, preserving the memory of this holy saint and his shining example of love, care and hospitality.

11

WHAT ON EARTH HAS HAPPENED?

Told by Martin Palmer
Written by Emma Geen

In Daoism it is believed that through meditation and living a simple lifestyle it is possible to achieve immortality. Unlike every other major religion, Daoism believes that immortality is not just for the soul. To be a Daoist immortal you don't just have to achieve immortality of the soul—you have to achieve immortality of the body as well. This is why this wonderful story has at its heart the need for a physical body. It is one of the canon of stories around the Eight Immortals. This group of misfits, eccentrics and reformed bureaucrats is like a combination of characters from the stories of Robin Hood and those of the Arthurian Legends. Li Tieguai in particular is seen as the friend of the outcast and the stranger and the cripple—for reasons which will become only too clear in the story.

This is a Daoist story about a handsome young man named Li Tieguai. Li Tieguai is as strong as an ox, has hair that shines like the sun and the heart of every woman who sets eyes upon him. What's more, he knows it.

Now, Daoism is unlike most other world religions, which believe that eternal life is achieved through leaving the body; for Daoists, no afterlife awaits beyond death, other than the continual manifestation of Dao. No, in Daoism, immortality is achieved in life and if you haven't got a body—a corporal soul—then you are soon bound for death.

Knowing this, Li Tieguai sets off up the mountain in his long powerful strides to begin his studies towards immortality. After all, as an immortal, ladies will be able to admire him, not just for a few scant decades, but forever.

So in a cave, near the peak of the mountain, Li Tieguai practises following the teachings of the founder of Daoism, Lao Zi. There he leads a life of self-discipline, undertaking tasks of religious devotion and resisting all temptations, be they woman, wealth or food, until, after ten years, his art is perfected to the point that he can travel astrally. This means that he can leave his body and wander the world as a spirit. However, there is a catch: he has to be back before seven days are over or his body will collapse and that will be the end of his immortal aspirations.

Now, Li Tieguai has a disciple called Li Jing. Li Jing isn't the brightest of disciples, but he's the only one who will put up with Li Tieguai's vanity and arrogance. For having always been smart, strong and handsome, Li Tieguai has little patience with those who aren't as lucky. But, ultimately, Li Jing is just glad to have a master, and Li Tieguai, though he'd never admit it, a disciple who hasn't left him yet, and so they muddle along just fine.

One of Li Jing's most important tasks is to look after Li Tieguai's body whilst he is away on his astral travels. It is a good arrangement, Li Jing gets to serve his Master without having to deal with his posturing for seven days and Li Tieguai can travel safe in the knowledge that a tiger isn't tucking into his physical form whilst his ethereal soul is elsewhere. He also knows—though he hates to even think of it—that should disaster ever strike, and he fails to return before the seven days are over, his body will be properly cremated.

So Li Tieguai sets out on his travels and Li Jing stays in the cave, watching over his master's body, washing sweat from its brow, making sure it's not too hot or cold and keeping a eye out for wild animals. Everything is going as it always does until the sixth day when a relative rushes up the mountain to say that Li Jing's mother is dying and that it is her last wish to see her beloved son one more time. What is Li Jing to do? Does he owe his loyalty to his master? Or filial piety to his mother?

What can he do? What can he possibly do!

Li Tieguai, meanwhile, has been having a fantastic time. He's travelled all over China, visiting all kinds of exciting and wonderful places. Overall, it's been a very satisfactory trip but now he's heading back. Being a show-off, he's cut it a bit fine, but he's still got half an hour to go. He's smart, strong and handsome, everything always works out just fine. What could possibly go wrong?

He swoops back into the cave…only to find it empty.

Where is Li Jing? More importantly, where is his body?

And so there Li Tieguai is, half an hour to go before the end of the seventh day, just standing, staring at what should have been his body for all eternity reduced to a pile of smouldering ashes.

Poor, foolish Li Jing. Torn between his two responsibilities, he had waited until an hour before the end of the seventh day, then burnt Li Tieguai's body and rushed down the mountain to say farewell to his dying mother.

Li Tieguai is gob-smacked. He is dumb-founded. Of course, he knew that Li Jing wasn't the brightest of disciples but he never expected this!

But time is running out.

'I've got to find a body.' He thinks to himself. 'I've got to find a body!'

As, if he doesn't, that will be the end of him. So he swoops down the mountain, searching and searching for anything to house his spirit, until he spies a recently dead body in a ditch. Perfect! He has only a minute to go, so without further ado he dives in. He's made it! And lying there, face down in the mud, he laughs in exhausted relief. That was close!

But then he tries to get up. And finds he can't.

What on earth is happening?

He tries again, but pain shoots up his arms and across his back. His legs can barely pull free of the mud. He's shaking all over. Something is very wrong indeed.

As you can imagine, Li Tieguai is extremely worried. But grabbing a branch, he manages to drag himself, hand over hand, painfully and slowly, very slowly, up onto his trembling legs, and from there straighten his back painfully and slowly, very slowly, into a stoop…but that's as far as he can go.

Now he's upright, he looks down the length of his body and sees that, beneath the torn, dirty clothes, his new legs are like saplings, the knees swollen knots. As strong as an ox in his original body, until now Li Tieguai has never even had to consider what it means to be weak. And so it is with growing bemusement, which soon sags into despair, that he tries to pull himself out of the ditch. The mud is so viscous and slippery, the slope so impossibly steep. Even climbing the mountain to his cave had never been as difficult as this.

It's only after an hour and much struggling that he finally manages to drag himself free. By now, he's close to collapse, but he's afraid that, were he to sit down, he'd never find the strength to stand up again. So, clinging grimly to his branch, he teeters on until he comes to a pond. What a shock he gets when he looks in! Not only has the strength of the ox abandoned him, but gone is his hair that shone like the sun, gone his allure to every woman. Instead the face that leers back has huge ears, straggly eyebrows and a matted, dishevelled beard. His posture is buckled over in a hunchback, his legs lame and gnarled. Only now does he finally sink to the ground.

He's repulsive! Deformed! And this is the body that he's going to have for the rest of eternity.

Of the adjustment period, I can tell you that it wasn't easy, though you have no doubt guessed as much. Smart, strong and handsome, Li Tieguai had always looked down on those without his good fortune, but now he is one of them.

Who is he without his strength? Who is he without his good looks?

Well, he still has his intelligence and though he no longer has the strength of an ox he is still as stubborn as one. What's more, he's started to learn the meaning of empathy.

And so he adapts. He turns his branch into an iron crutch and, though irascible from the pain, he continues his studies, hobbling on as best he can. It is from this crutch that he comes to gain his name—Iron Crutch Li. Those who do not know who he is, treat him as a freak, a beggar, a stranger and often set their dogs on him or their watchmen. Through this he comes to really understand that the stranger, the outsider, needs to be cared for and he sets this as his goal: namely to defend the weak, the poor and the rejected by bringing down the mighty and the haughty and teaching them compassion.

Almost as infamous as his crutch is the gourd bottle he carries with him, for in it, it is said, is a liquid panacea that can cure any sickness. And so Li Tieguai becomes known for travelling around, curing the sick and aiding the outcast, whom, through his new body, he has finally come to understand.

So Li Tieguai joins the infamous Eight Immortals and becomes the great guardian of the needy and the oppressed. There are many fabulous stories of the tricks he plays upon the powerful and the wealthy in defence of the underdog, but these will have to wait for another telling.

12

ALL THE RIFFRAFF

Anna Conomos

Saint Philaret was an Orthodox Christian who lived in the 8th century in the Paphlagonian district of Asia Minor—in modern-day Turkey. He is known as Saint Philaret the Merciful to denote his amazing compassion and generosity to all—friend or stranger—and to distinguish him from Saint Philaret of Moscow.

"You're bringing WHO to stay this time? Some poor miserable wretch from the slums no doubt...and who's left to clean and cater for all of your fly-by night guests! Me! But you don't think of me do you? Everyone else yes, but your wife is always last...I have no privacy, no time to myself with all these stragglers you keep bringing home. And the smells! The rudeness that I have to put up with! I have no room to move..."

This was the daily rant that erupted in the home of Philaret. His name, you know, means "lover of virtue". Unfortunately, his wife did not share the same love and

indeed every virtuous act on his part was always greeted
with a tirade of objections...

"It's always the same story with you...*she* has been travelling for days, can we keep her? *He* has no shelter for the
night, can we take him in? *They* have a baby, shouldn't we
feed them? There is no peace, no space, no respect for me
in my own home!"

Actually their home was the grandest and the most
spacious residence in their district. It was a magnificent
building, a real landmark in the town of Amnia, a city in
Paphlagonia which was a prosperous and busy corner of the
Byzantine Empire. Philaret himself was a wealthy landown-
er with extensive fields, flocks, beehives...and many

servants to run the estate. As such, his wealth attracted a lot of attention…but by all the "wrong people", according to the missus. "At least if they were emissaries from the Imperial and Sublime Court of Constantinople—that would be all right, but you bring me all the riffraff!"

Constantinople: city of a thousand domes and capital of the greatest Christian Empire, was at this time under the regency of the Empress Irene, mother of the young Emperor Constantine VI. It really was a breathtakingly magnificent place, admired by all the world. Its palaces, hippodromes and cathedrals straddled the shores of the gleaming and busy Bosphorus, a strait connecting the Sea of Marmara to the Black Sea. Whenever Philaret would travel there on business, his wife would insist on joining him, eager to make some new and expensive purchases and to gossip with the other aristocratic ladies who would enter the shaded double-tiered arcades in purple sedan chairs. She would pretend not to look when Philaret stopped in his tracks to offer food to a hungry beggar and she would stare in silent contempt if he chose to invite lonely travellers along the way to join them for a meal.

"Why couldn't we live in this Queen of Cities instead of in our mundane old town? We could be out every evening dancing to music or taking boat rides along the Bosphorus. Why couldn't you have been a Bishop or an Archbishop? I'm sure they get paid well with all those fancy clothes they wear; imagine how pretty I could look by your side."

"Bishops don't marry dear; they dedicate their lives to the service of the church and the faithful," Philaret would answer wearily.

"Oh. Well, God clearly approves of wealth. Look at the gold on all of His churches; the immense cascade of domes; the fine mosaics and frescoes that cover every wall. Isn't there a bit in the Bible about rich people entering the Kingdom of Heaven on a camel?"

"We've been through this before, my dear: 'It is easier for a camel to enter the eye of a needle than a rich man the Kingdom of Heaven.'" Philaret would often have to correct his wife's interpretation of the scriptures, which she would always tailor to reflect her own interests.

Philaret himself found daily inspiration in the writings of the Bible and every morning he would read and re-read passages from it to his two eager granddaughters, Mary and Maranthis. They would listen with wide-eyed delight to the stories of the righteous Abraham who welcomed three strangers into his home only to discover that they were three angels in disguise; stories of the widow of Sarepta and the woman of Shunem, one received prophet Elijah, and the other Elisha, into her home and witnessed miracles such as the dead being raised, tales of Jesus Christ who always singled out the poor, needy and homeless. "*Pappou*, grandfather, perhaps the poor people are angels!" the girls would say. Thus inspired, Philaret would get down on his hands and knees and raising his arms up to the skies, he would say: "Lord you have blessed me abundantly with fields, vineyards, flocks, servants and a grand home. Please show me how I too can be like Abraham to be sent angels that I might welcome into my home."

And God heard Philaret's prayers. But instead of sending him angels and prophets, he sent beggars, exiles, the lame and widowed. For every field Philaret gave away God replaced with two more; for every animal, God gave him four more; for every item of food, God re-filled his storehouses to bursting. Soon Philaret's fame spread throughout the Empire and far beyond it.

But one day, God decided to test Philaret's faith. On a dark night, a fierce gang of robbers stole into the little town of Amnia. And since Philaret's house stood taller than any other, since the sound of his sheep and oxen and donkeys was louder than in any other farmyard, since his fields heaved with corn and fruit trees more than in any other pasture, since Philaret's wife had draped precious carpets and ornaments across the balconies for all to see and admire, they carried off anything they could lay their hands on, wreaking devastation in their wake and leaving Philaret and his family with nothing but a donkey and a handful of bees.

Now you can imagine the horror and outrage that broke out the next morning in the town of Amnia! You can imagine Philaret's children and grandchildren crying with fear. You can imagine the servants and the farm hands packing up their bags and, in disgust, setting off to find better employment elsewhere.

You can imagine the mistress of the household tearing at her hair, screaming, "What's to become of us! We can't live on honey! Philaret! Philaret!"

And you can imagine Philaret, on his hands and knees with his arms reaching up to the Heavens, praying his usual morning prayer, "Lord thank you for…for…"

"Philaret!" Only this time, if you had looked closely, you

might have been able to notice his hands betraying a slight quiver, his eyes filling with fear…

"Philaret!"

"…don't abandon me Lord…"

"Philaret!"

With every hysterical shriek Philaret prayed even louder, clenching his fists, choking back his frustration, bowing his head with despair…"show me what to do; *what should I do?*"

And all at once he remembered a story from the Scriptures: that of the righteous, long-suffering Job. He had lost not only his riches but also his family, yet he kept his sights so focussed on God that he was finally rewarded with great prosperity and a long life… "He lived to the ripe old age of two hundred and forty, long enough to see grandchildren and great grandchildren…" Philaret muttered. And that was it! Philaret picked himself up with renewed energy and an unburdened heart. "I'm coming my dear!" he chuckled, and stepped out of his room, as lively as a grasshopper chasing a gnat. His whole countenance shone with peace, full of smiles; no-one could believe their eyes. And that afternoon, when he came across a poor peasant bewailing the loss of a donkey, Philaret promptly handed over his own without a second thought.

His wife fainted on the spot.

From that day on, she confined herself to bed on account of a bad headache and digestion problems. But despite all this, Philaret would urge his family to be patient and they would soon reap the rewards.

Sure enough the day came when two emissaries really did come from the court of Constantinople. Their mission

in Amnia was to find fair maidens from a good family; one would be chosen as a wife for the young Constantine. On that day both headache and acid reflux miraculously vanished and Philaret's wife was the first to run into the street offering hospitality to the two travellers. "You see, I'm learning!" she said to her astonished husband. Observing that Philaret's residence was the most splendid in the town, the envoys agreed to spend the night there. Philaret's home soon filled with villagers and townsfolk, all turning up to offer a plate of something for the newly-arrived guests who surely were tired and hungry after their long journey. And of course they all brought their daughters and granddaughters along to help carry the plates of food and to serve. But out of all the beautiful, fresh-faced maidens that had gathered, two stood out: Mary and Maranthis, Philaret's granddaughters. They had been so trained in virtue by their grandfather that the spiritual beauty of their souls enhanced their physical beauty and they easily prevailed over all other contenders. Their minds freed from doubt, the envoys escorted the damsels to the imperial court and presented them before the Emperor Constantine, who was enchanted. He took Mary to be his wife and united Maranthis to one of his principal courtiers. He then summoned Philaret and the rest of his family to the palace where he raised Philaret to the rank of consul and gave him more riches than he had ever had before.

For the first time his wife was speechless.

But Philaret did not allow this newfound wealth to overwhelm him. He immediately prepared a sumptuous feast to which he invited the homeless, the poor, the old and the disabled of the city. He spent his days wandering through the streets carrying three purses: one full of gold, one laden with silver and one bursting with copper coins. Whenever he came across beggars he would dip into his purses and shower coins over them. On one such day, Philaret's wife decided to join him and she too dipped her hands into the purses. She held the coins in her fists for just one moment before releasing them into the air over the begging crowds, and for the first time she felt truly happy.

And so the years passed peacefully until the day that the merciful Philaret knew his death was at hand. He gave away the last of his remaining goods to the destitute and needy and when his work was finished he crossed himself and lay down to rest. He called his whole family to his bedside and rested his eyes on each of them, one by one, "*Tekna mou*, my children, please remember my words and keep them in your hearts. Do not forget hospitality; visit those who are sick or in prison; watch over the widows, strangers and orphans; see to the burial of those who die in poverty; attend the services of the church; do not wish for another's goods and never speak badly of anyone or rejoice over their misfortunes; always do as you have seen me do in my life so that God will keep you under His protection." And with that he gave up his soul to God and his face radiated with joy and light, having lived the words in the Lord's prayer, "Thy will be done on earth, as it is in Heaven."

13

MY CLOTHES WERE WELCOME

Jumana Moon

Nasrudeen is a much-loved figure from folk tradition in many Muslim countries. He is based on a character who is thought to have lived in the 13th century AD in what is now Turkey. He was a teacher who used humour to help people enjoy and therefore understand the profound truths about life contained within Islam.

Nasrudeen is mercurial and changeable. He is known by many different names: in Arabic countries he's known as Joha or Goha, in Kenya as Abu Nuwas. In Turkey they call him Nasrudeen Hodja and in Pakistan and Iran Mullah Nasrudeen. His stories have even travelled to Muslim China. Sometimes he is a judge, sometimes a layman, sometimes a preacher, Imam or Mullah. He shifts in time too—that is his chameleon nature. There are stories about him from the court of Tamerlane, other stories are unfixed in time and there are still contemporary stories being made up about him, now. One thing does stay the same—the way Muslims from Algeria, Iraq, Turkey or Pakistan smile and chuckle when a story about him begins or his name is mentioned. His stories always involve what appears at first to be strange, even idiotic behaviour. But through it he highlights the idiocy of the rest of us! Nasrudeen: a foolish wise man or a wise fool? That, my friends, is up to you!

One day Mullah Nasrudeen was passing through town when he saw that a rich man was holding a great banquet. Through the open door of the house came bright, warm lights, the sound of people talking and laughing—and there also came the tempting wafts of good cooking. Nasrudeen could not resist and so he presented himself at the doorway, where a couple of servants stood as doorkeepers for their master's feast. That night the Mullah was wearing his usual clothes—a rather tatty plain *qamis*, the long ankle length all-in-one shirt that Muslim men in many countries wear. I'm sorry to say it wasn't easy to tell what colour his *qamis* was supposed to be—perhaps it had once been white though now it was a shade of dishwater grey and it bore a good many stains and patches. Nasrudeen's turban was not faring much better and was also not of the long, fashionable length but was rather short and frankly, quite lowly as turbans go. His sandals were cracked and broken and as he walked the strap flapped and flicked with an irritating "slap".

So when Nasrudeen presented himself at the doorway the servants looked him up and down. One of them burst out laughing and the other waved his hand at Nasrudeen and told him to go away. There was no way he was coming into this fine banquet.

Nasrudeen went home. Perhaps it was the bright, warm lights or the delicious smells, perhaps it was just Nasrudeen's way, but he looked through all his cupboards

and chests. He found a fine robe, much grander than a
qamis, in a beautiful shade of blue, with brocade buttons
and fine, wide sleeves. He found a long, broad length of
cloth, which he wrapped into a fabulous turban, high and
stately—far more suitable for a Mullah of good standing.
Finally he found a pair of soft leather shoes, with elegant
turned-up points at the toes. He walked out of his house—
then he quickly turned back, went back into his house, put
some water on his moustache and twirled it, 'til it looked
sleek and black—then he was ready to go.

Nasrudeen went back to the banquet—this time the
servants smiled and swept him a low bow, holding out their

hands—"welcome, welcome do come in!" The Mullah went into the banqueting hall and sat down on a cushion at a low table. The dishes and drinks were being passed round. First of all, Nasrudeen took the jug of *sharbat*, an excellent drink, flavoured with pomegranate seeds, tamarind and cooled with snow from the high mountains. He took the jug and poured a good glug of the *sharbat* into one wide sleeve of his robe (he gave a little shiver at the snow, as it was rather chilly). Then he picked up the soup and poured a generous helping into the other sleeve. As someone was passing the roast chicken round he picked up a drumstick and tucked it neatly into the folds of his splendid turban. Then he took

the stew pot from the middle of the table and tipped several spoonfuls down the front of his robe.

By now the host, in a terrible fluster, came dashing up to Nasrudeen, just as Nasrudeen was reaching for the finger bowl of water scented with rose petals—and we will never know where Nasrudeen was intending to tip that as the host grabbed his arm. "Mullah," he hissed, "what are you doing? You must stop, you are embarrassing me before my guests."

The Mullah looked at the host and replied, "Well, as it was my clothes that were welcome at the banquet, it seems only right and fair that it is my clothes that enjoy the eating and drinking of it!"

14

A CRACK IN THE WALL

Vayu Naidu

This story is similar to ones found in many religions. Namely that God will favour the outcast or the poor person, whom the religious authorities despise and dismiss. In such stories as this, it is the miraculous movement of a religious statue that signifies divine delight in the simple worship of the devotee, over the ostentation of the wealthy people, who think that their riches are why the God should favour them. Kanakadasa is a real pilgrim who began life as a warrior and later became a great poet, philosopher, musician and composer. He is said to have lived for a hundred years from 1509 to 1609.

Kanakadasa had travelled far under the wide coastal sky of south Canara to Udipi. He wanted to see his beloved Krishna, the god who had saved Kanakadasa's life on a battlefield when all sense of humanity had been lost. He arrived in Udipi late at night and slept under the sky. He woke early in the morning and washed himself by the temple tank.

He stood in the queue, clean but bedraggled, his head keenly leaned forward over the long row of pilgrims' shoulders as he strained to see the doorway of the inner sanctum. It would be quite a while before the line of pilgrims chanting the thousand and one attributes of Krishna could enter the temple and pay their salutations to the guardian deities of Ganesha, the bringer of peace, and Garuda, the eagle father of the skies. "Govinda, Krishna, Mukunda, Nandalala, Madhava, Madhusudana, Keshava..." the murmurs and chants filled the senses. Hundreds of secrets of the human heart whispered from hundreds of pilgrims, each voicing their secret longing to God Krishna.

Kanakadasa's only longing was to see Krishna directly, to have his *darshan*. All his calling out to Krishna was a "thanksgiving". He remembered the time he had been in battle. He belonged to the herdsman caste and was their chieftain. His opponent was fierce and nearly cut him to pieces. But suddenly, his enemy dropped his sword and

fled. That night Kanakadasa dreamed of Krishna as the charioteer on the battlefield, the way it was in the epic Mahabharata. At last he was here in Udipi to see the deity of Krishna, shown as a young boy, eternal, playing his flute and weaving a canopy of love to all mankind.

As Kanakadasa shuffled along in the queue, he tripped over the heels of the pilgrim in front of him. This immediately caught the attention of two priests. They pounced on him and declared that anyone so clumsy was not worth being in the line of worship. They asked Kanakadasa what his caste was and contemptuously raised an alarm. As he was not of the priest caste he should be banned from seeing the deity. He would only be allowed a perambulation and then he could face the western wall at the rear of the deity. They called the temple guards and instructed him to be thrown out as he was a beggar and had no learning about how to worship. They tied his arms above his head and Kanakadasa was made to stand facing the wall at the rear of the shrine.

Kanakadasa, being the poet and singer that he was, broke into song as the other pilgrims shuffled along:

"O Krishna, You who are the infinite sky, the colour of blue
You who are space within and without
How could You hold a wall between us?
Did you not save Prahlada from his egocentric father in the
    form of a lion?
Did you not save the river from the poison of the serpent and
    tame its ways?
Did you not save Draupadi from disgrace?
O Krishna of the magic flute, in what way can a man like me,
    born without choice into caste,
See you, only You?"

While everyone's hearts were moved, the Brahmin temple priests did not give in, as it had become a question of pride and a mark of their authority.

Kanakadasa's words flowed like honey.

Suddenly, there was a crack in the rear wall, the stones started falling out, and the Krishna deity turned around from its original position of facing east, to face west where Kanakadasa was imprisoned. The crack in the wall became a

window, and with streaming eyes, Kanakadasa saw his
beloved Krishna.

Every year on the twenty-fourth of November there is a
celebration to mark this event of Kanakadasa's victory of
ardent faith over ignorance. And since then many pilgrims
from all castes can now see Udipi Krishna.

15

THAT'S JUST MY LAUNDRY

Adele Moss

Herschele Ostropolyer is the Jewish equivalent of Nasrudeen and stories about him often contain the same basic format and punchline. Herschele however has a more mischievous element to him than Nasrudeen, as is clearly spelt out in this story. The Jewish tradition of hospitality to the stranger is contained in many such folk stories. For example, at Passover, the festival which commemorates the liberation of the Hebrews from slavery in Egypt, any stranger who is hungry is invited to the ritual supper. How could one celebrate freedom without remembering the hungry and the oppressed?

Apparently the original Herschele Ostropolyer, who came from Ukraine and lived from 1757 to 1811, was a jester at the court of a Hassidic rabbi, Rabbi Boruch Mezbizher. The rabbi found it hard to be as joyful as Hassidic philosophy demanded and hired Herschele to raise his spirits. According to the folk tales, the rabbi often forgot to reward Herschele for his pains, forcing him to wander from village to village, begging. This story comes from the Yiddish folk tradition.

Ukraine once had a large Jewish population and the vibrancy of Jewish religious and cultural life that once existed in that part of the world needs to be remembered. In spite of waves of extreme persecu-

tion culminating in the Nazi extermination plan and subsequent immigrations, there are still Jews in Ukraine. Yiddish folktales from many parts of Eastern Europe have been collected and archived. They appear in various publications and some are still told in Jewish communities or studied and recounted in the original by Yiddish speakers and students.

There was once an old woman who owned an inn. She was rumoured to be lacking in generosity, though she would put it differently. "I run a tight ship," she would say with pride and her customers had to agree. Perhaps they would have liked to decamp to a more generous establishment, but hers was the only guesthouse in the neighbourhood. She would serve wild nettle soup, which cost her next to nothing. But even then, on dishing up the green liquid into earthenware bowls, she would have second thoughts and ladle some back into the pot.

One dark, wet afternoon, when it looked unlikely that she would have any customers, at least until the rain stopped, she was just making her way to her bed for an afternoon nap, when there was a loud knocking on the door. She was expecting a very distinguished guest in the evening, but he certainly wouldn't arrive in the rain. Grumbling, she went downstairs and was most put out to find a beggar on her doorstep. He looked a terrible sight. His soaking wet hair emerged from his dirty torn cap in rats' tails; his greying shirt clung to his bony arms, his trousers were done up with string and his shoes gaped to reveal his big toes protruding through his socks.

"What do you want?" she snapped.

"Just a place by the fire to dry out and perhaps a bowl of soup and a piece of bread, if you can spare it."

Herschele Ostropolyer, an itinerant well known on his home patch, Mezibisz, made it his business to research the standard of local hospitality by consulting other travelling beggars. He already knew that if his hostess possessed any shred of generosity, it was deeply hidden.

The old woman understood very well that this guest would not be paying for his meal. It occurred to her that the stove was lit and it wouldn't cost her anything to allow him to rest in the kitchen. But as for free food…

"What a shame," she said, "I've just run out of everything and I won't be going to the market till tomorrow, so no food, I'm afraid. You can sit by the fire for a bit, at least until it stops raining."

She showed Herschele to the kitchen and waved to a bench by the stove. Herschele put down his pack and heard a noise, a gentle clatter, the noise of a lid happily bouncing on its pot as something simmered, something fragrant. Why, he would recognize that smell anywhere. It was boiled chicken.

"Madam," he said. "Could you have forgotten that you have some chicken cooking, maybe soup?"

The old woman reddened and snapped:

"That's just my laundry. I'm boiling handkerchiefs. Isn't it strange how boiling laundry often smells like chicken?"

With that she stomped out and upstairs to her bedroom.

Herschele lay down on the hard bench and tried to sleep. The fire was warm but his empty belly refused to be comforted. The heavenly smell reminded him of his

mother's soup. Now what did she put inside it? Chicken
wings and carrots, garlic and onions…

"I'll just take a quick peep at this 'laundry'." He took off
the lid and there was the chicken fat melted on the top of the
fragrant liquid and, yes, chicken wings and drumsticks. He
found a large spoon. "Just a taste…what's this, a wing?
Delicious. Shame to leave a chicken with only one wing,
might as well have the other one. Oy, whoever heard of a
one-legged chicken? Better eat this leg too. A limbless
chicken? No, better eat the lot. I'll just chase this slippery
onion…"

Soon the only thing left of the dish was the liquid and the bones and Herschele was fast asleep on the bench, dreaming sweetly of his mother in the kitchen, dishing up endless food.

"Wake up, wake up, I've got a guest."

He opened his eyes, murmuring "Mamale" and was shocked to see the hard features of the innkeeper.

"Hurry, hurry, you've got to go. It's stopped raining."

Herschele picked up his pack and made his way to the entrance hall, where a finely dressed gentleman and his footman were taking off their coats. Before they could greet Herschele, the old woman whisked them away into the kitchen and sat them down at the table.

"You must be very hungry after your journey. Here, I've been simmering these chickens all afternoon. Would you like to help yourselves?"

She had put a damask cloth on the table, her best porce-
lain and the large pot. She gave the gentleman a large silver
serving spoon and fork. He took the lid off, dipped the fork
in and extracted a sopping grey rag, down which a few bones
slithered slowly back into the pot. The landlady screamed
and pointed at Herschele, who was just trying to exit quietly.

"It's that stinking beggar!
He's eaten the chicken.
Stop, thief!"

"Madam," said Herschele, "You said you had no food in the house and that you were boiling laundry. I thought you wouldn't mind if I added my vest."

The gentleman stared open mouthed for a second and then burst out laughing. He rose from the table and said to his footman: "If there is one thing I can't stand, it's meanness. Let's travel on and see if we can find an inn where they also feed the poor. Herschele, why don't you come with us?"

The gentleman gave Herschele a lift to the next crossroads and enjoyed listening to one or two stories of his exploits on the way. When they parted company, he gave him some money to help him on his travels.

PART FOUR

MODERN

16

THE PROMISE

Anna Conomos

This story is set in 1922 when, during the Greek-Turkish War of 1919 to 1922, the city of Smyrna was captured by the Turkish Army. It tells what happened to a city where Christians and Muslims had lived side by side for a thousand years or more. It was created by Anna Conomos for the 2012 cross-media project 'Twice a Stranger', run by the Greek multimedia production organisation Anemon about the greatest forced migrations of the twentieth century, when millions of people were uprooted and moved to new homelands.

O nce upon a time there was a beautiful girl called Evgenia. She was seven years old and she had a best friend with jet black hair, starry eyes and a voice like an angel; her name was Fatma.

They lived in a cheerful little village, full of walnut trees and orange groves, the village was set high on a hill overlooking the great and glittering seaside city of Smyrna in Asia Minor, which is in modern-day Turkey. Greeks and Turks had lived in this village side by side for hundreds of years, the Greeks on one side and the Turks on the other.

The two girls loved each other dearly and they wanted to do everything together but this wasn't always possible because Evgenia was Greek and a Christian while Fatma was Turkish and a Muslim. This meant that during the week they had to go to different schools, on Sundays Evgenia would go to church while on Fridays Fatma would go to the mosque, and in the Spring Evgenia would celebrate Easter with her family while Fatma would celebrate Ramadan with hers.

But even though their families had different habits and practices, the girls tried to spend every possible minute in each other's company; in the morning they would go to the orange groves and watch the sunrise and listen to the peal of the church bells, after school they would play together in

the square and listen out for the muezzin's call for prayer, but best of all they loved the moment when the sun would sink into the distant sea and the old town crier, Barba Ioannis, would take out his oud, pluck at the strings and sing their favourite songs...

> And what do you care where I am from,
> From Bournova or from Kordelio?

Evgenia was a wealthy little girl, she lived in a grand two-storey home which her mother would proudly refer to as their "*arhondiko*", their mansion. It had a balcony wrapped around the bottom floor, large windows to let in the sunlight and palm trees on either side. Her father owned acres of land with vineyards and fig trees and apricot trees. He would dry the fruit and take it in great big carts down to Smyrna and from there it would be shipped out across the sea to Greece, Italy, Spain and to the rest of Europe. Sometimes Evgenia and Fatma would ride on the fruit carts, chew on the juicy fruit and spend the day on the quayside admiring the boats and wondering what sort of world lay across the water. Evgenia had heard a lot about Mother Greece, from her priest and school mistress; it sounded like a wonderful place, but she had never been there, she had never been anywhere outside Smyrna, but she was fine with that; for Evgenia there was no better place in the world than home, where life was perfect.

But, one day, war came and *everything* changed: the church bells stopped their regular ringing, the muezzin stopped his melodious calling and Barba Ioannis could no longer be heard playing his oud…everyone was tense and anxious, Greeks and Turks became suspicious of one another and shut themselves away. Evgenia couldn't understand who or what war was, but she didn't like it because no one was being normal anymore…and the worst of it was that Fatma no longer came to play.

"Mama, I want to go and see Fatma."

"My dear, you can't."

"But you like Fatma don't you?"

"Of course I do, but things have changed now."

So now Evgenia had to spend most of her time at home, indoors; it was so annoying. One evening, she heard her parents arguing in the kitchen, her father was shouting, which was strange because he never raised his voice...she pressed her ear against the door.

"The Greek army has left, the Turkish army is coming...we should go tonight, we're not safe here..." Mother was crying.

"But there are all those ships in the harbour, the British ships will save us won't they? I'm not leaving my home, this is *our home!*"

Leaving! Leave home? Why? And without saying goodbye to Fatma? No way! Evgenia was going to see her even if it meant disobeying her parents! She crept out of the house and past the church, she ran through the village square, everywhere was strangely empty and quiet. She ran past the orange groves and noticed that the sunset was in a different place tonight, further back and it was flaming red, brighter than ever before, but there was no time to lose, she kept running all the way to the Turkish quarter, past the mosque and then turned the corner; there was Fatma's home and there was Fatma on the terrace.

"Fatma! Fatma!" Fatma ran down to meet her friend and the two girls threw their arms around each other.

"Evgenia, I'm not allowed to play with you anymore, you're a Christian and not a Muslim like us, and...I heard Mother say that war is coming...oh Evgenia, I don't know who he is but he sounds horrible!"

"Fatma, quickly, listen to me, we have to make an oath...It's like a secret promise which you have to keep forever even after you are dead, OK?"

"OK."

"We have to promise that no matter what happens, even if this war comes and takes us away from each other, that we will come back one day and meet right here under the terrace at sunset. Promise?"

"I promise!"

To seal their vow Evgenia plucked a rose from a nearby bush and they dug a hole in the ground, placed the rose in the hole and then they hugged with all their might, the tears freely flowing down their cheeks.

Suddenly whistles were blasting, bells were ringing, the town crier was shouting for all Christians to leave their homes, people started to fill the streets. Before Evgenia knew what was happening she found herself being scooped up and carried off in someone's arms until Fatma was a tiny speck in the distance. She recognised her father's voice.

"What were you thinking? How dare you run off!" She could feel his heart beating hard against her chest. When

they reached the outskirts of the village, mother was there, waiting for them with blankets and food.

"Oh Evgenia, thank God you're alright! Take my hand and hold on tight!"

Now for the first time Evgenia could smell smoke in the air, she looked behind; there was fire, fire everywhere and she remembered the sunset...or what she thought had been the sunset. More and more families were gathering from all the neighbouring towns and villages, she could see girls from church and school but she couldn't see Fatma anywhere! Mother took her by the hand and now they were running downhill, people of all ages all running at top speed towards the city of Smyrna, screaming: "The soldiers are here!"

Old grannies were falling and no one was stopping to pick them up, babies were screaming, Evgenia's legs were aching.

"Mama, I'm tired, Mama..."

"Come on, don't slow down or I'll lose you forever!"

Finally they reached the quayside, behind them a furnace of flames, in front of them the sea, the whole place was heaving with people. Evgenia hummed to herself to block out the sounds of screaming and choking and frenzied panic around her.

But now she could hear a different music. A strange music she had never heard before, it was a woman's voice, it sounded so funny. It was coming from those big foreign battleships, lots of them all along the harbour...why weren't they coming to rescue people? Why were they just sitting there! So people were jumping into the sea trying to get to them, but they must have grown tired of swimming because

they just ended up lying face down, bobbing on the surface of the water. Evgenia felt herself being pushed closer and closer to the edge, it was so hot, she was thirsty, she couldn't breathe! "Mama, mama, mama!"

And then everything went black.

When she opened her eyes she found herself in a little fishing boat in the middle of the ocean, her parents were there, some people from school and Barba Ioannis was there, too, with his oud tucked into his jacket. She wasn't sure how many hours or days had passed but then she saw light from the flames on the distant shore and sounds of people still screaming, she thought of Fatma, of home, of the rose and in her nails there was still the fresh earth from home…so far away, so very far away…

They travelled for days and weeks, stopping off at different ports, crowded into camps with thousands of other refugees and then starting up again. The journey felt endless.

"Where are we going?" Evgenia would ask her mother.

"We're going to Greece. To Thessalonika. We'll be welcomed there, it will feel like home, you'll see." But when they finally arrived at the port of Thessalonika, there was no welcome, the locals didn't want them there, they called them *"prosfiges!"*—refugees—and put them in camps; their home was not a grand two-storey house but a pokey half-made tent that smelt of death and disease! They hadn't eaten for days so father had to go and find work, but it wasn't picking fragrant fruit and shipping it to the rest of the world, now he was sweeping the dirty city streets and he would come home at the end of the day with his clothes dripping in sweat, dirty and frustrated. And one evening, Evgenia saw him cry for the very first time—"Over there we lived like kings and now look how low we have sunk! I'm not even making enough money to buy a loaf of bread for my family!"

Time passed and soon the word began to spread that the war had ended and that there was now peace! Hurray! The refugees started to pack their belongings with joy! They could go back home now! Evgenia and her family went back to the port of Piraeus and there were many boats waiting there, but they were not waiting for them. They were being loaded with other refugees. Evgenia noticed among them girls her age, they looked like Fatma with beautiful jet black hair. They were carrying blankets and food, people were shouting and whistles were blasting. "All Turkish Muslims ready to board." And the people were crying and getting into the boats...so now the Muslims were being made to leave their homes in Greece and go to Turkey. They had been swapped!

"I want to go too!" cried Evgenia. "Please swap us back again! This isn't fair!"

But they had no choice. In time the Greek refugees were moved into a neighbourhood where they built little huts for themselves to live in and they called it "Neo Kordelio" so that they could remember their homeland. Of course it was nothing like home, but sometimes in the evenings, Barba Ioannis would bring out his oud and the people would ask him to play songs from the homeland and he would pluck the strings and sing...

> And what do you care where I am from,
> From Bournova or from Kordelio?

And the refugees would forget their pain and remember happier times.

The years passed and Evgenia grew up and married and had children and then her first grandchild was born, a little girl, and she was given her name, Evgenia. Now little Evgenia loved her grandmother and especially loved listening to her stories. They were always about a magical, beautiful paradise that granny would call her *"patrida"*, her homeland. Granny would tell her of orange groves and songs in the square but she would always cry when she spoke of a wonderful girl, called Fatma, with jet black hair and starry eyes and a promise they had made to meet again.

But granny couldn't keep that promise, she got very old

and sick...and on her deathbed she took her granddaughter by the hand and said "Evgenia, will you do something for me? Will you keep my promise for me?"

"Yes, Granny, I will." And then she closed her eyes and died. Little Evgenia never forgot granny's stories or her songs or her promise and years later, when she became a young woman she took a boat and crossed the seas to Turkey to see her grandmother's paradise. She reached the port of Smyrna and was amazed at the beautiful city; some of it looked as though it had been destroyed by fire. As she made her way uphill she came to a mountain village called Guledge, which in Turkish means "village of roses". And when she saw it, it was as though she had known it all her life. The grandest house was a huge two-storey mansion with bay windows and a balcony wrapped around the bottom floor. It was just as granny had described it, she really had lived like a queen. Here was the old church and the square and the orange groves...the sun was just beginning to melt into the distant sea, she followed the path and saw a mosque, turned the corner and saw a sight that made her gasp in amazement: an enormous bush climbing up a terrace, full of roses, dozens of them in full bloom! Evgenia's heart began to beat wildly, she knew this was what she had been looking for, she buried her face in the flowers. So it wasn't just a story! This was real. A gentle voice made her start. It was a young lady with jet black hair and starry eyes, she was smiling at her; she spoke in broken English.

"Those were my grandmother's roses, they were very special to her."

"What was her name?"

"The same as mine...Fatma."

"Fatma? I am Evgenia: these roses were special to my grandmother, too."

The two girls stared at each other and hesitated for just one moment before grabbing hold of one another and embracing, laughing and crying at the same time. Then Fatma reached out, plucked a rose from the bush and held it out.

"Take this to your grandmother from mine, it was her dying wish."

"That's very kind, Fatma, but my grandmother died, some time ago."

"Then you must place it on her grave."

So Evgenia took the rose and then the two girls put their arms around each other and went into the house. It was as though they had known each other their whole lives.

17

SO STRANGE

Victoria Finlay

In 1934, a four-year-old boy was abandoned outside the Sikh Gurdwara in Lahore, in what was then India and is now Pakistan. He was severely mentally and physically disabled: deaf, mute, and also incontinent. Puran Singh (1904–1992), who was later given the honorific title Bhagat ji, was working as a volunteer at the Sikh Gurdwara in Lahore, inspired by the Sikh teaching of service and the examples of compassion to strangers of the Sikh gurus. When he saw the child he picked him up, washed him, named him Piara, meaning beloved, and from then on treated him as his adopted son, carrying him in his arms or on his back almost all the time. The end of British rule in India in 1947 led to "Partition", when India was divided into India and Pakistan. Puran Singh and Piara moved as refugees from Lahore (now in Pakistan) to Amritsar, the Sikh holy city now on the Indian side. There they founded an institution called Pingalwara, which still cares for strangers and the destitute. He ascribed the establishment of this centre entirely to Piara. "If Piara had not come into my life, or if there had been an institution in 1934 which could take care of Piara, I would have sent him there. But then there would have been no Pingalwara!"

The night before my third child was born, a fortune-teller came to the door. It was a cold night and she was hungry. My older brother, whose wife was also about to give birth, didn't want her to come in.

"We're busy tonight, sister," he said. But I said she might bring good luck.

For a bowl of dal lentils and three chapati flatbreads she went into a trance. Just a little trance, mind, only so much as a small bowl of dal and three thin chapatis were worth.

"The girl will be a good wife; she will marry a man in another country," she said, and then she spilled words about eyes like stars and fine fingers for fine embroidery, all meant to get a few extra annas from us. But then she said something so strange.

"The boy will be responsible for a great institution; his photograph will be taken and shown around the world and they will write stories about him even in a hundred years. And he will never do a wicked deed; he will never say a wicked word." And then she added: "And yes, he will save his father's life."

After she had gone, my wife and my brother's wife just laughed and laughed. Their bellies were so big that night that we were just waiting to see who would give birth first. From the beginning my wife had been sure hers was a girl. We had two boys already and this one so different in the womb.

"She's so patient, she's not kicking, just stroking me from inside," she'd tell me in that last month. I didn't mind a girl so much. And my wife didn't say, but I knew she wanted someone to keep her company.

My brother's wife? Well this was her first, though they were married before us, and she was praying for a boy. "When my son is a famous man we will eat well and live in a huge house near the Lahore Fort," she said. "And we will eat *gulab jamun* sweets every day, and you can come and live with us too." And all that night our wives sat up and talked in low voices spinning stories of riches and power and the future, to keep their minds off what was going to happen. And even when the births had started—both in the same hour—and the Dai nurse had been sent for, they were still laughing about the fortune teller. None of us believed it of course, and yet if it were true...

My brother didn't stay; he went out until morning. Me, I went for a walk, but soon I came back, tired of watching my breath in the grey light. It was hard to know who was screaming hardest behind the door, and then a higher wailing came. The Dai opened the door.

"A girl," she called out. I stood. "No, not yours, your brother's," she said. I knew he'd be upset. He wanted a son.

My wife's screams kept coming. And then there was silence. Someone was sobbing very quietly. I could hear the street waking up outside. I knocked and there was no reply. It was not right to go into a room when another man's wife had just given birth. But I pushed open the door. My sister-in-law was crouching with a baby in one arm, her other hand stroking my wife's forehead. The Dai was facing away from them with something in her arms. It seems like a photograph you see in a newspaper to me now, in greys and black and white.

"Can I see my child?" I asked. The Dai turned around. She held something that wasn't a baby. It was like a fawn in the forest, all spindly legs and long arms. And it was silent. My other two had yelled to the heavens when they were born.

"What is it?" I asked.

"It's a boy."

That wasn't what I'd meant.

My brother called it "it" and said it was disgusting. He said we should get rid of it.

"It's a boy and he's my son," my wife said. But we didn't give it a name. My wife called it Bachcha, which means "young thing", and as she cleaned up after it she said, "you will be famous"; as she wiped its mouth she said, "you will be responsible for a great institution"; as she held up its head, which couldn't hold itself up, she said, "you will be photographed; you will be greatly loved."

My brother said my wife was crazy and my son was retarded and I knew everyone agreed.

We couldn't afford another mouth, but we really couldn't afford one that couldn't talk or cry or eat without drooling, or clean up after itself. Even if we could afford a servant-girl it would have been hard to find anyone to look after it.

I got into the habit of talking about my two sons, not three, and sometimes I'd ban her from looking after it. Anyway, I knew she'd go to it when I'd gone out, and in a way I was glad.

"He'll save your life one day," she'd say. And foolish girl, she seemed to believe it.

Bachcha was four when my wife died.

The first week my brother's wife looked after it or pretended to when I was around. She cut its hair very short; said it was easier to look after it that way. But at the beginning of the second week when I returned, Bachcha wasn't there and nor was my brother.

"Where is it?" I asked when he got back.

"It's safe enough," my brother said.

"Did you sell it as a beggar?"

"No. Though I should have, now you suggest it."

I was better off without it, for sure. But every time I went out in Lahore to work or to walk I found myself looking.

And in the Partition in 1947, as my two sons and I were swept up along with *lakhs* of other people and driven from our homes to become strangers in our own land, to my surprise I found myself still looking. It would have been sixteen.

Then we fled over the new border.

And in the refugee camps on the India side and then in the Hindu temple that gave us shelter over the border, and then in the Sikh Gurdwara in Amritsar where I found myself without a rupee to my name, and where they gave us food, thousands of us every day, I kept looking for it. I didn't want it back; I just wanted it to be safe.

Then I had an accident with a truck on the Grand Trunk Road. My leg was almost torn off, I was barely conscious. They took me to the hospital, pulling me on the back of a rickshaw but I had no money. Who did in those days? Then they picked me up again.

"Pingalwara!" someone said.

What's that?

"Home for cripples."

I passed out on the journey but I was awake when they dragged me up through the main gate. It was new, square, there was a courtyard and there were people laid out everywhere on the ground. I must have passed out again, because when I woke up, my leg was bound up and a nurse was checking the wound.

"You were lucky," she said. "Bhagat Puran Singh ji was here today. He touched you and prayed for you; you will get better now."

I pulled myself up as well as I could. "Who is he?"

"He's over there," she said. And in the distance, bending over a woman so thin she was almost invisible, was a tall man in a brown shawl, with a grey beard and deep eyes. On his shoulders was a strange package wrapped in a blanket. I couldn't see it clearly, but it looked like a bundle of sticks.

"What's that thing around his neck?"

"It's a boy! He's so famous I'm surprised you haven't heard of him," the nurse laughed.

"He can't walk, so Bhagat-ji carries him everywhere. He can't speak or hear, but Bhagat-ji says he's blessed. He calls him Piara Singh, Beloved Lion."

"And how did he come to Pingalwara?"

"They say he was abandoned in Lahore, outside the Gurdwara. His family must have wanted to get rid of him, and nobody in the Gurdwara knew what to do. But as soon as he saw him, Bhagat-ji just picked him up and they have been inseparable ever since. Bhagat-ji says he would never have started Pingalwara without having Piara to look after. We say he was our first stranger."

But he was not a stranger to me.

He was my son.

18

THE LION

Told by Sef Townsend
Written by Emma Geen

This tale comes from the Jews of Ethiopia, who were airlifted to Israel during the Great Famine of Ethiopia in the mid-1980s. This famine inspired Live Aid, a pop concert held in 1985, which raised millions of pounds worldwide for those who suffered from the famine and was in itself a modern expression of compassion for the stranger.

This story was told me on the banks of the Sea of Galilee. It was June, the water was a brilliant azure and the air sang with cicadas and the sweet scent of flowers.

I was talking to a woman called Yuvi Tashome, who was telling me about her experience as an Ethiopian in Israel and her work trying to help young Ethiopians find opportunities in Israeli society. I knew the background to her story as I had been in Sudan in 1984 when the Ethiopian famine was in full force. I had met lots of Ethiopian refugees and loved their music, the melody of their voices, their clothes. Of course, many of them were starving but even when you're starving you're still proud. So I met them, I listened to their songs and shared their food when they had food to spare.

Now, the traditional Ethiopian dish is a flat, fermented, cake-like bread, called *injera*, but what really makes it special is the practice of cooking and serving it in one large pan, around which everyone will sit and eat as a family. This setup not only brought people together, but as the parents ate first, or a sick person if one was present, it was a subtle way to educate the children.

While I was there, the Israelis decided to airlift the Ethiopian Jews to Israel in what was known as Operation Moses. Yuvi had been one of those Jews and her life changed very quickly when she arrived in Israel. One of the things she missed most, however, was the *injera*, as in Israel there weren't the big pans needed to cook them. The Israeli response to this, ever pragmatic, was: "It's OK, just cook them in small pans." And so the Ethiopians started to cook their *injera* in small pans, and each person had a half, or their own individual *injera*, and along with this, as has happened in our society, people stopped sitting down to eat together. The tradition that had held the community together had disappeared. Now, many years later, Ethiopians in Israel are either making their own large *injera* pans or importing them into Israel and Yuvi hopes that this will bring people back together. Let's hope she's not too late.

When Yuvi finished, we mulled quietly over our

thoughts, but after a moment she lifted her head once more, and she said:

There once was a princess.

The King, the father of the princess, thought that it was time for his daughter to get married and so he appointed all the eligible young men—royals and foreign princes—from far and wide to come and woo her. Well, people came, people went, royalty in their beautiful carriages, nobles on their proud stallions, poorer men marching in their Sunday best. Until, one day, along with the princes, came a lion.

The lion stood before the father of the princess and said, "I've come to ask for your daughter's hand. I hope she'll like me. After all," he touched his chest with a muscular paw, "I *am* a king."

During this speech the father of the princess had sat up in his throne.

"Well, yes," he said, eyebrows rising as he regarded the lion. "I can see you're a truly magnificent beast, but—" and he hesitated as his eyes came to rest on the lion's rugged, golden mane. "My daughter is a very tender, delicate person. If I were to introduce you as you are she might get frightened by your wild hair. Could you do something about it? Perhaps cut it a little bit?"

So the lion went away, and not only did he *cut* his mane but he *tore* it out, and *pulled* it out, every last whisker and bit of his mane so that he arrived at the palace the next day a completely bald lion.

Well, the King rubbed his chin and passed his gaze over the lion once more.

"I see that you made a great effort." the King said. "I'm sure now that my daughter won't be at all frightened of you when you—" but again his voice broke off, for his eyes had now fallen upon the lion's paws. "But, I mean if you were, for example, to embrace her…you've got rather sharp claws. Don't you think you should file them? Or cut them? Just a little?"

So the lion went away, but instead of filing his claws, he *tore* them out from the *root*, he *yanked* every claw, from *every* paw and when he presented himself in the throne room once more his limping steps left spots of scarlet on the marble floor.

"There is no way that I will hurt your daughter when I embrace her now," he told the King.

The King lent back in his chair with a satisfied nod. "Well, that's wonderful! You look much better and you're not going to hurt her if you embrace her—" but his enthusiasm vanished as he looked upon the lion's teeth. "But, well. Don't you think your teeth are rather sharp? If you were to kiss her you might accidently...*bite* her mouth, or...or put a little mark in her cheek, and that would be truly terrib—"

But the lion had already turned away, and rather than filing down his teeth he *pulled* them out from the gums, *every last, glistening* tooth, and when he dragged himself back, to plant himself before the King, his muzzle was pink with bloodied saliva.

"Nou." The lion's cheeks puckered in pained breath. "Nou, I canno' hur' her a' all."

The King rose from his chair. He looked down his dais at the lion, who stood staunch before him, but without his mane, without his teeth, without his claws, and the King's expression broke into disgust.

"Do you really think my daughter would want to marry a cat?"

Oh, the lion was so angry, but what could he do? He could try to pounce on the King but without his mane he couldn't frighten him, without his claws he couldn't scratch him, without his teeth he couldn't bite him, and it was very easy for the King's servants to simply drag him from the room. And so the lion slunk from the palace, and left without his mane, without his claws, without his teeth...and without the princess.

*

Yuvi stopped her story there. She didn't need to say anything else because what she was saying was clear. "When we came to Israel we were lions, but what are we now?"

19

SISTER AGATHA'S MOBILE

Told by The Reverend Sister Agatha Ogochukwu Chikelue
Written by Emma Geen

Sister Agatha is a Catholic nun who lives in Nigeria and is one of the most dramatic, charming and generous of nuns you are ever likely to meet. This story was one of the tales told one evening in Nairobi, Kenya, when the Stories of the Stranger *team held a storytelling evening late into the night.*

Jesus was once asked which commandment was the most important. He replied it was the one about loving God, but then added that the second most important was: "Thou shalt love thy neighbour as thyself." Because charity is what Jesus teaches us, no? He loved everyone and so he helped everyone, whether they be man, woman, child; poor or rich; virtuous or unworthy.

But the problem with being charitable is that sometimes people abuse it. And so there are times when I get confused and I don't know whether to go on being generous or not. And I say this as a woman who is a nun.

See, I come from Abuja. Abuja is known as the best built city in Africa, and easily one of the wealthiest. Here, you see businessmen walking round the cool fountains of Millennium Park in smart suits that would cost a poorer man his year's wages, or driving cars that could feed a whole village for the year. And so for many people in Nigeria, Abuja is a catchment area. Everyone is trying to move here. The feeling is that anyone who lives in Abuja is like, "Oh, we've made it. We've found our place in this world". And so some of the people who come to our city, if they see anything they want, they just try to grab it. Because of that you tend to get many stories. Some stories that are not true, but many that are.

So it happened that we have been getting people coming into the parishes or our offices, asking for one help or the other. They are of all sorts, women, men, maybe even a little girl. But after a while the stories they tell all start to sound the same.

"Sister, Sister," they say. "I have travelled far from home to visit my uncle in Abuja. I called him on the phone and he said that I should come and that he wants to give me some money to start a business. But on arriving I realised that my uncle is no longer living at the address that he gave me. Now I am confused and I don't know what to do."

The first time I experienced that, I gave the person what I had to give. Yet back at the convent, sharing the story with my sister, she shook her head.

"How were your eyes?" she said. "Because these people, you just don't know."

And she was right, but still, how do you turn away someone who might be in real need?

And so this is how I thought until one day, when a lady with a little baby came to my office. She just walked right through the convent, opened my door and moved straight on in. I was working on my computer at the time and so I was like: "Uh uh?"

These people, they don't know it's wrong to barge right in.

"Aah, Sister," she said, "I'm so sorry."

So I was like, "It's no problem. What can I do for you?"

"Oh Sister," she gushed, "they have demolished my shop, at the garage, in fact I don't know what to do. Assist me now, Sister. This is why I carry my baby, my husband—he has run away, and I have another two. I don't know, I'm going back to Suleja, it's one hour from Abuja, and I don't have a dime with me to go back. I don't know what to do."

Is this sounding familiar?

But her baby looked like it must only be, maybe, three months old. It was tired and restless, so I was like, "Madam, please, sit down."

So she sat down and started breastfeeding her baby. I didn't have much money but, having heard her story, what I had I was happy to give her. I knew she might be telling the truth, or she might not, but I thought, let's give this to her for the sake of the baby.

She was still breastfeeding when I handed her the money, but the moment I handed it over she stood up.

I cried out, "Madam, why are you rushing? Sit down and finish feeding your baby. When you are finished, then you can go."

And she was like, "Hey, Sister, I don't mind. This baby, he just needs a suck."

And I was like, "Madam, why are you in such a hurry? Relax and breastfeed your baby."

But she was like, "Oh Sister, her little brothers are outside and I have to meet them when they come."

So I was, like, "OK, no problem."

And she left.

About five, ten minutes went by, when I wanted to make a call, so I started looking for my phone. After my last call, I put it on top of my table but I could no longer see it. So I keep on looking, looking, underneath the desk, in my pockets, down the back of the chairs, but I can't see my phone anywhere. Now I'm getting really worried, because my phone is not just a phone to me, it has all my contacts in it and I don't know what I'd do without it. So I have to rush

to my neighbour and borrow her phone to call my number and see if my phone fell somewhere I hadn't thought of. I get back to my office and start ringing, but it keeps on telling me that "the number you have called is not available".

It was then that I realised—the woman with the baby.

So I was like, "Oh my God, how terrible can people be?" I was trying to help this lady and she walked into my office just to steal my phone. But I had to get my SIM card back, so kept on calling, calling, all through the night.

"The number you have called is not available" it tells me, "the number you have called is not available", again and again and again, until I had called twelve times that night, and, suddenly, the dial tone rang.

A man picked it up. "Who are you?" he says, and he is clearly very angry.

So, I said, "Please, look I am so sorry. Good morning, sir. I am begging you, in the name of God, can you just drop my SIM card anywhere I can collect it, please. Just the SIM card, I'm begging you."

"Wrong number," he snapped, "no call this number again." And put the phone down.

That is what these people are like.

Oh, I could have cried. I had lost my phone and all because I was trying to be charitable. This is what I get out of being generous, I thought, and after all else that I'd done. Jesus might have taught people to love their neighbours, but no one ever stole his mobile phone.

I was angry for a while, it was difficult having lost all the information on my SIM card, but eventually, I realised that I shouldn't let what happened with one woman change my beliefs. Sometimes being charitable and hospitable takes a little sacrifice, but that is why we have to work at it. It is hard, but it is the right thing to do. And so I still believe that none of what these people do should discourage us. It should not.

20

THE SHADOW OF SHAME

Told by Sef Townsend
Written by Emma Geen

This is a traditional Korean story reworked by Sef Townsend and Sharon Jacksties. It is told by Sef Townsend who tells stories in special centres working with refugees from all over the world, including asylum detainees who are held in Campsfield Immigration Removal Centre in the United Kingdom, a long-term centre where detainees are accommodated, pending their case resolutions and subsequent removal from the United Kingdom. Detainees from centres like this throughout Europe are often sent to countries where they may well have an extremely unpleasant reception and could even face death. Sef says refugees respond very well to this story. They say: "This is our story…We come here to make a good life. Not just for ourselves, but to share with the people we live among."

This story is about a young man who escaped from North Korea to the South. The journey is a treacherous one, many attempt it and many fail, so when he succeeded, the young man seized hold of his new life with eagerness.

"I'm going to fit in," he told himself. "Even though people speak differently here and I sometimes struggle with what they say, I will try my very best. If I am good and hard-working, surely people will warm to me."

Yet, for all this goodwill, it was not to be. Like many in his situation, most people in the South treated him with scorn. To their eyes and ears he spoke differently, he looked different, he *was* different. However, the young man had not come so far only to give up, and so all through that first sultry summer, he travelled from village to village in search of a new home.

One day, entering such a village, the young man saw a huge chestnut tree. The day was hot and he was weary from his walking, so he settled himself into its shade and found it so deliciously cool that before he knew it he was asleep.

"Hey!"

A brusque voice startled him awake.

"Hey!" The voice demanded again as the young man blinked into the sun's glare. "Get out of my shade!"

'Did he really say get out of my shade?' the young man thought. 'Perhaps I have misunderstood.'

So he sat up and raised a hand to his eyes so that he could peer at the harsh silhouette of the man standing over him.

"Excuse me, sir. Please, could you say that again?"

"Stupid foreigner," the man spat. "I said get out of my shade!"

Now that the young man's eyes had adapted, he could make out the supercilious sneer of the man's face and knew that he had understood him perfectly the first time. Yet he was still puzzled.

"But, sir, doesn't shade belong to everyone?"

"*My* grandfather planted this tree and if he planted this tree it's *my* tree, and it's *my* shade." And with every "my", the man stabbed a digit into the palm of his hand. "SO GET OUT OF MY SHADE!"

Knowing a lost cause when he saw one, the young man hauled himself to his feet. He stuck his hands into his pockets and prepared to slouch away, but as he did so he felt the smooth shape of coins and, as he really was loathe to leave the shade, he was struck by an idea.

"Sir," he said, "perhaps I could buy this shade from you?"

The man threw his head back in laughter and when he finally choked it back he had to squeeze his words out between tears of mirth.

"50 won." He laughed. "It will cost you 50 won."

Of course, the young man knew that this was an extortionate amount, but as he traced the shape of the coins in his pocket, he found he had five big 10 won coins and one little one won coin—just enough. He cupped them in his palm and felt their weight as he studied the man in front of him, who was obviously well dressed and had had a lot of good meals. The young man could not afford such expense, and the rich man could easily spare it, yet he found himself handing the money over.

The rich man's eyes went wide as he took the money, perhaps in delight, perhaps in disbelief, but he didn't question the young man's decision, after all, he had just made a tidy sum out of nothing.

"OK, sit in the shade then!" he said, and returned to his house still laughing.

So the man settled back beneath the tree and returned to his doze, but—as you know—when the midday sun moves one way, the shade moves the other, and so the shade moved across the road and into the beautiful garden of the rich man. Well, the young man didn't want to trespass but as he was now the owner of the shade he went into the garden, lay back on the lush grass, and fell asleep. But not for long because—

"GET OUT OF MY GARDEN!"

The young man rubbed the sleep from his eyes. "But, sir, you sold me this shade."

At this, the rich man clenched his fists, but what the young man said was true, so he stamped back inside his house and slammed the door.

But still the sun moved, still the shade moved, off the grass and onto the generous balcony just outside the house where there were plush cushions and comfortable chairs. So the young man hopped up, took a chair and cushion, and returned to his nap.

"GET OFF MY VERANDAH!"

"But, sir." The young man lifted the pillow that had been shielding his eyes. "I'm just enjoying the shade that you *sold* me."

And so the rich man retreated inside his house, his face the colour of blood.

And so on the sun moved, and on the shade moved, and on the young man with it, through the sliding doors of the balcony and into the lounge.

Now the rich man broke.

"GET OUT OF MY HOUSE!" he bellowed in a spray of spittle. "YOU ARE TRESPASSING! POLICE!"

And before long the police were there.

"What's going on here?" the officer asked.

"He's trespassing in my house." The rich man grabbed the young man by his shirt but the policeman kept his calm and turned to the young man.

"Sir, would you like to explain what's going on?"

"I'm in his house, yes," the young man said. "But only to stay inside the shade that he sold to me."

The police took off his cap and rubbed his bald head. "I'm sorry. Could you explain again?"

"He sold me the shade," the young man said. "Under

normal circumstances, I would never dream of entering this house, but my shade is here."

"Is it true that you sold this young man the shade?" the policeman asked the rich man.

The rich man fidgeted with his fine clothes but could not look the policeman in the eye. He'd been found out and in Korea shame is a big deal.

"Would you mind telling me, sir," said the policeman, "how much you charged him?"

"Uh, uh, well, um, 50 wo…"

"50 won!?" the policeman shouted, loud enough that the neighbours could hear.

"Horrible old man," they cried over the fence, "selling shade! Always doing horrible things!"

The rich man was so embarrassed, so ashamed. He held his head down and walked out of his house, across the verandah, across the lush grass, past the chestnut tree, and on round the corner out of the village. After all, he had many other houses.

Well, with the commotion finished, all the onlookers went home and the police returned to their station, leaving only the young man.

I'd better stay here and make sure that no burglars take over the house, he thought. Because even though the rich man had treated him badly he felt guilty to have caused him shame. So he stayed there the night. But in the morning the rich man still hadn't returned.

The young man walked about the house looking for signs of him and, as he did, he noticed some torn paper in a window—you see, windows in old Korean houses were made of paper—and he patched it up. When he had finished, he cast around and, seeing that the house was in poor repair, he might as well keep going. So he swept the floors, tidied the kitchen and replaced some broken roof tiles.

But at the end of the day there was still no sign of the rich man, nor after two days, three, four, five, six, seven...So the young man thought he might as well see to the garden and planted some seeds.

A month went by, and still the rich man had not returned.

Two months, still no sign.

On the third month the first radishes and lettuce were ready for harvest but as the young man was picking them, he looked up and saw the hollow cheeks of the poor people of the village.

"Here," he told them. "Have some radishes, have some lettuce." And he started handing out the goods from the garden. "While you're here why don't you come and help me? If we all dig we can produce more and share."

The villagers thought it was a good idea and so they did just that. The villagers dug, the villagers cleaned, harvested, planted, watered. It was a hive of activity.

Then autumn came, and still the rich man had not returned. Looking down the road for a sign of him one day, the young man's eyes fell on the tree that had started it all and saw that its chestnuts were ripe.

"Let's go and pick the chestnuts," he said to the villagers.

"Oh no, we can't do that," came the reply.

"What do you mean?"

"He never allows us to pick chestnuts."

"But where is he?" the young man said. "He's not here. What harm can it do?"

And so all the people climbed the tree, plucking chestnuts to toss into their baskets and singing to make light of the work. Amongst all this festivity no one noticed a man slinking up the street, his head held low, only looking shiftily from the corner of his eyes. So it wasn't until he was right beneath them that a lad up the tree cried out.

"Uncle! Hey! Welcome back."

The rich man looked up at the smile of the lad and saw that it was genuine, he listened to the people's singing and heard that it was joyful, then he saw the young man to whom he had sold the shade all those months ago, his arms spread.

"Welcome, sir. We've been looking after your house while you've been away. Come in."

The rich man followed him in a daze. The garden buzzed with the happy sounds of the people tending to the vegetables but when they saw him, instead of breaking into frowns, they called out greetings.

"Uncle! Welcome back."

"As you can see," the young man said, "we've been looking after the garden for you, sir. We've been keeping the house together too. So, now, welcome back to your home!"

But at the threshold the rich man stopped and stared long and hard into the far distance until people began to think something wrong. But at the young man's query, the rich man held up a hand, and when he finally spoke his voice was weak.

"I can't possibly take this house back. You, in six months, have done more than I have done in my whole life. I've never seen my people smiling or laughing like this. Never once has anyone welcomed me. But you transformed this place. Please stay and look after it in my name. It would make me very happy."

And that's the story of the Shadow of Shame.

CONTRIBUTORS

Benaifer Bhandari is a storyteller and poet who loves to share the ancient beauty of her Zoroastrian faith. Her background as a home-opath, gives her an inherent interest in humankind, their struggles and the way in which anyone can turn the energy of struggle into the energy of hope. She lives in Hertfordshire with her husband and two autonomously educated sons.

Gordon Brown is a British Labour Party politician who was the Prime Minister of the United Kingdom and Leader of the Labour Party from 2007 until 2010. He previously served as Chancellor of the Exchequer in the Labour Government from 1997 to 2007. A Member of Parliament since 1983, first for Dunfermline East and currently for Kirkcaldy and Cowdenbeath, in July 2012 he was named by Secretary-General Ban Ki-moon as a United Nations Special Envoy on Global Education.

The Reverend Sister Agatha Ogochukwu Chikelue is a Nigerian Catholic Nun from the Congregation of the Daughters of Mary Mother of Mercy. Sister Agatha is currently the Director of the Archdiocesan Liaison Office, Co-Chair of the Nigeria Women of Faith Network, and the Secretary of the Interreligious Dialogue Office of the Catholic Archdiocese of Abuja. Sister Agatha holds a B.Sc. in Public Administration and an M.Sc. in International Affairs and Diplomacy. She has shown a keen interest in promoting peace and dialogue in Nigeria especially among women from different religious groups and tribes, and also in their environmental problems.

Anna Conomos, international storyteller, writer and actress, is of Greek origin. Born in Canada, she spent much of her early life in Australia and Greece before moving to the UK. In 2005 Anna won the Young Storyteller of the Year UK award. Anna delights in bringing to life myths and songs from across the globe and giving them a contemporary twist! She has performed in festivals, museums, at conferences, on boats and on rooftops in Greece, Holland, Australia, America, Romania, Russia and the UK.

Victoria Finlay was an arts journalist in Hong Kong for 12 years. In 2002 she published her first book, *Colour* (Hodder & Stoughton), which included journeys to Afghanistan to find Michelangelo's expensive blue paint. Her latest book, commissioned by the Getty Museum, Los Angeles, will be published in September 2014, called *A Brilliant History of Color in Art*. She has worked for the Alliance of Religions and Conservation (ARC) part time since 2004, as communications director. She first heard the extraordinary story of the founding of Pingalwara during a visit to Amritsar in 2010 as part of her role as an advisor to EcoSikh.

Emma Geen is a speculative thinker and writer who is fascinated by the power of narrative to shape reality. Her first attempt to mould the cosmos, aka her debut novel, is a body-jumping and mind-mangling examination of the human condition, which will be published by Bloomsbury in 2015 and won the 2012 Janklow & Nesbit Prize. She is endlessly captivated by the strange and wonderful workings of sentient human beings, and, alongside her

MA in Creative Writing from Bath Spa University, holds an MA in European Philosophy and a BSc in Psychology.

Katriana Hazell is a curator and producer based in London. From 1997 to 2009 she was Cultural Director of Asia House, London and prior to this was at the Commonwealth Institute, the National Museums of Scotland and the Scottish Arts Council. Since 2009 she has worked with the Alliance of Religions and Conservation (ARC) as a consultant on artistic events including producing *Hearing the Voices of Creation* a major performance at Windsor Castle in 2011. She was project manager for *Stories of the Stranger*.

The Reverend Eustace Kabue was born in 1960 in Nyeri, around the Mount Kenya region. He is a wonderful teller of stories, not just from his Christian faith but from his African heritage. He has studied in both Kenya and South Korea. He serves as a minister in the Presbyterian Church of East Africa (PCEA) and has also served as a college tutor, university lecturer/chaplain and is currently secretary to the Mission Board of the PCEA. In 2009 the PCEA church started the Environmental Stewardship and Sustainable Agriculture Committee, putting it under its Mission Board which has gone on to collaborate with the Alliance of Religions and Conservation and the All Africa Conference of Churches in Nairobi, Kenya.

Jumana Moon is a psychotherapist and storyteller with a particular love of sacred and traditional stories from her Islamic faith. She tells stories in schools, places of worship and at community events. Jumana loves stories because they are graceful, funny and compassionate ways to relate to people, especially where there is difference, fear or conflict. She feels very privileged to regularly be able to listen to and share stories with storytellers of other faiths, an exchange that she feels continually enriched and enlightened by.

Adele Moss grew up in a family of German Jewish refugees, nourished by constantly evolving stories. She has a background in drama and has worked as a storyteller in Oxford for the past twenty years in many different settings: schools, day centres, theatres, libraries, museums, hospitals, religious and interfaith groups, to name a few. She uses stories from all around the world, but always returns to Jewish sources, which she revisits with a contemporary resonance. She is particularly interested in the capacity of stories to create connections between people of different backgrounds and ages and is enriched by her current storytelling partnership with Muslim storyteller, Jumana Moon.

Dr. Vayu Naidu studied oral narratives and traditions of performance from the Indian subcontinent and did a comparative analysis of western experiments of theatre by Peter Brook as her doctoral dissertation at the University of Leeds. She founded the Vayu Naidu Storytelling Theatre Company, funded by Arts Council England from 2004-2012, collaborating and commissioning on Storytelling of World Epics for Intercultural Audiences and Education. Vayu's first novel, *Sita's Ascent*, published by Penguin in 2013, is an original work of fiction following from her storytelling theatre performance of the Ramayana. She is currently Sage in Residence at Eton College.

Martin Palmer is a storyteller, broadcaster and writer, and heads the Alliance of Religions and Conservation (ARC) which he founded with HRH Prince Philip. He is a well-known translator of Chinese

Classical texts such as the Dao De Jing and the Shang Shu. He is a religious historian and theologian.

Ranchor Prime, who designed this book, worked on ARC projects before starting a small London-based publishing house, Fitzrovia Press. He designs, illustrates and writes books on spirituality and ecology, and teaches yoga and mantra chanting.

Sef Townsend does much of his work with refugees and people in exile. Through the medium of storytelling and story sharing (mostly using traditional tales) a safe way is found of speaking the 'unspeakable', enabling the refugee storyteller to feel that their voice is finally being heard. When not working in mosques, synagogues, meeting houses, churches and interfaith and cross-cultural projects throughout Britain, he is involved in peace and reconciliation projects in Northern Ireland, South Africa, Israel and Palestine, where an attempt is made to address conflict through creativity and through striving to find that which is truly equal and human in each of us.

Sylvia Woodcock-Clarke is an extremely old lady who has drawn and painted professionally for all of her adult life. She attended Camberwell School of Art. She was awarded a major county scholarship and received an NDD at the end of her course. She exhibits mainly in the Middle East where she has lived for the last decade. Three years ago she injured her right shoulder in a fall and was unable to paint so she turned to illustration. She has illustrated several children's books including *Panic in the Clinic*, published in 2011 by Milamant.

ACKNOWLEDGEMENTS

This book was made possible through funding from the Ministry of Foreign Affairs of the Norwegian Government under their Refugee/Migrants programme. We are very grateful for their support and encouragement.

Our thanks too to all those whose skills and knowledge as story-tellers have made this project possible. They include the London Group who met to tell each other their stories and delight in each others' traditions; the people at the Values, Beliefs and the Environment Channel of UBrain TV who recorded them; the Nairobi Group who met in September 2012 to laugh and joke as the stories tumbled out. Our thanks also to our colleagues at EcoSikh for their fast contribution of background information for the Sikh story. Special thanks to Emma Geen for her brilliant writing, Sylvia Woodcock-Clarke for her powerful drawings, Gordon Brown for his generous introduction, and Ranchor Prime for his beautiful design. And finally thank you to Anthony Weldon, and his keen-eyed colleague Dominic Horsfall, for having faith in us and in being one of the most engaged and engaging publishers we have ever worked with.

Martin Palmer and Katriana Hazell

The Alliance of Religions and Conservation (ARC)

ARC was founded in 1995 by HRH the Duke of Edinburgh. Its mission is to help major religions around the world develop and carry out their own individual environmental programmes, because—in different ways—their own core teachings, beliefs and practices all have nature at their core. ARC also works with key environmental organisations to help them link with religions, creating powerful alliances between faith communities and conservation groups.

Stories of the Stranger was developed with funding from the Norwegian Government.

"If you believe in God...then you should feel a responsibility to care for His Creation"

HRH The Duke of Edinburgh, founder of ARC

www.arcworld.org

Other inspiring titles produced in collaboration
between Bene Factum and ARC

FAITH IN FOOD
Changing the world—one meal at a time
Edited by Sue Campbell and Susie Weldon

"Never doubt that a small group of thoughtful, committed individuals can change the world, indeed it's the only thing that ever has."—*Margaret Mead, American cultural anthropologist*

The Alliance of Religions and Conservation (ARC) has come together with representatives of six of the world's major religions (Buddhism, Christianity, Hinduism, Islam, Judaism and Sikhism) to shine a light on how we deal with one of the most important parts of our lives—food. Eating is a moral act: our choices of what, when and how we eat have a huge impact upon the Earth, our fellow human beings and other living creatures.

Faith in Food is a unique vision, combining essays, scripture, story-telling, recipes, initiatives and general wisdom in this beautifully produced book, all seeking to challenge and explore our relationship with what we eat, and how we obtain our food.

In the foreword to *Faith in Food*, HRH Prince Charles, The Prince of Wales, says:

"The world is waking up to the fact that we have to find ways to produce food more sustainably because of the enormous challenges facing us. With accelerating climate change, rising costs of fuel and fertiliser and a rapidly growing global population, we need to ask whether the way we produce our food is fit for purpose in the very challenging circumstances of the 21st century. We simply cannot ignore that question any longer."

He concludes: "Our sacred traditions can lead us back into a 'right relationship' with the natural world and restore a sense of reverence for the food that sustains us, the creation that provides it and for the noble profession of farming, the very foundation of a healthy civilisation."

Paperback
ISBN: 978-1-909657-41-0
Price: £14.99

What began as a casual acquaintance with Daoism on a business trip to Taiwan in the late 1970s ultimately led to a collaboration that has helped this ancient Chinese faith be one of the most environmentally active religions in the world. In *Sacred Mountains*, Allerd Stikker shares his remarkable journey through the world of Daoism. He shows how Daoism survived near annihilation in the 20th century and how it has regained its place in the heart of Chinese culture. Its close links with nature and its ability to guide and inspire people on the path to making China cleaner and less polluted are now acknowledged by the Chinese authorities as well as Daoist communities. The sacred mountains display a rich biodiversity thanks to the care and eternal wisdom of the Daoists, who today are a key factor in balancing ecology with economy in the world's most populous country.

Mesmerising artwork and expert contributions round out a sweeping blend of history, spirituality and politics, that relates how these made the past and will shape the future of both China and our planet.

Hardback
ISBN: 978-1-909657-56-4
Price: £14.99

Visit **www.bene-factum.co.uk** to find out more about
all the other great books we have to offer